Calling All

Earth

Angels

&

Healers

Coauthored books with Geri Magee, Ph.D.

Success Breakthroughs
Jack Canfield, 2018

Warrior Women with Angel Wings:
Illuminate Your Joy
Sundi Sturgeon, 2018

Warrior Women with Angel Wings:
Gleaning the Positive from the Negative
Sundi Sturgeon, 2019

Reading Between the Signs:
Anthology of Signs and Synchronicities
Jill Rhiannon, 2019

Grandma in the Box
Geri Magee Ph.D. 2019

<u>Theorist</u>
Geri Magee, Ph.D.

Universal Relationship Pyramid
http://Www.UniversalRelationship.com

Calling All
Earth
Angels
&
Healers

Compiled by Geri Magee, Ph.D.

"With the universe in her wings, Earth Angel gently cradles our precious world, bearing gifts of tranquility, harmony and peace for all. In her wake, she brings an abundance of beautiful flowers and creatures great and small to fill the idyllic countryside. The dove of peace and the rainbow of hope are her constant companions on her flight of creation."

Available as a limited edition Giclee' at www.josephinewall.co.uk Prints come with a Certificate of Authenticity signed by the artist.

Calling All Earth Angels & Healers © Geri Magee, Ph.D.
First Edition, 2019
Printed in USA

ISBN: 978-1-7097516-5-3
Imprint: Independently published

Cover Design and Editing: Karen Tants and Geri Magee

Cover artwork: © Josephine Wall. *"The Three Graces"*
Used under license

Acknowledgments

A very special and grateful "thank you" to my designer, editor, and newly found friend Karen Tants, for aiding me in my first compiled book adventure. She is my "Wizard of Words", without her support this book would not be possible.

To my best friend and love, Magdy Salem, for supporting me throughout the years, while I reinvented myself and adapted to be a functioning disabled woman finding her way and restarting life once more. For this, I am eternally grateful and thankful to my Higher Power for giving him the strength to support and care for not only me but also both of our families.

To my children, I thank you for being supportive of me in my new endeavors as an author and mom who just can't be in every place at the same time. I am so proud of how each of you has developed to be loving, kind parents, friends, and humans.

To my mother, I am eternally grateful for the life you gave to me while growing up, the sacrifices you made along with work and dedication; as a single parent in the 1970's, it was not easy. You gave us the values to have in order to uphold in society and you have instilled in us to be proud of who we are in our own right. To my siblings, thank you for everything, especially keeping me in the loop.

To my grandchildren, human and furry, for being the light that ignites my soul each time I think of you. You will forever be the apple of my eye.

To Bruiser (my pet rat). My dearest and closest companion over the past three years. You will be forever loved and cherished in every aspect of my mind, body, and soul. I am so grateful you came into my life by divine guidance when I most needed you. I cherished the moments that we were able to snuggle together. You are dearly missed but forever part of my soul.

A special thank you to Jack Canfield™, Patty Aubrey™, John Assaraf™, Jared Yellin and Jake Ballentine; not only are you my colleagues, mentors, and guides for the last three years, you are also my friends. Your ongoing encouragement throughout my health issues kept me going when I thought I could no longer live and with the systems you have available I was able to beat all the odds. You are all Earth Angels and Healers to so many. May your wisdom and dedication to your field be carried on for eternity.

To my immediate family, I thank you all for your encouragement and loving support. You are always in my heart and prayers.

To my adopted family (very close friends), without you, I don't think I would have been able to get this far. Thank you for being by my side and forever in my heart. I thank you for the loving support we have given each other throughout the years.

To my friends online and in groups, I treasure you. Day or night someone out there would inspire me to keep fighting for my soul. Any time I needed an uplift or good cry, I could turn my computer on (which I hate lol) and scroll through all the pages, which had such beautiful words that kept my soul on fire. Once I was well, I started to do this for others and I have now a great group of likeminded/soul friends that we have built a great online community for those who are in need.

To my coworkers, coauthors, colleagues, and associates, I commend you for the hard work and ongoing dedication to your fields of expertise. How you inspire not only others but also yourselves on a daily basis encourages me to keep going each day.

With many blessings and deepest love, Geri

Preface

As a healer for many years now, people have often asked me, "what is an earth angel?". One can be both an earth angel and healer, the main difference in some is the belief system of one's own self. For myself, I believe I am both. Having multiple roles that I have needed to use throughout my life for myself, family and others, I have noticed either a significant overlap or have experienced a 'complimented balance' to what I was doing in order to keep mind, body, and soul together.

There are many practicums whereby you do play roles as both an angel and as a healer. For instance, there are religions that teach healing within their doctrines, and there are many careers that utilize either the religion or the study of science as the foundation of their belief system or practice, and most definitely there are many that remain separate entities, including the roles you play in them whether for spiritual or financial gain. On the other hand, there are careers that do not allow a belief system to be involved, but that should never deter you from finding that outside of your career for balance.

Now, many of you reading these co-authored stories and definitions may find yourself reflecting on where you are now versus where you want to be or need to be for one reason or another. However, that does not mean you will not still be able to find a balance for yourself on your own life's journey.

You will find in the back of the book the stories I co-authored in other authors' books. The reason I choose to add them to this book is that each story builds upon the next in each subsequent compendium. This gave me great insight into the literary industry; I would call each submission a trial run of my own comfort zone to learn about my capabilities. I learned so much over the past thirty-six months since the beginning of being invited to co-author with Jack Canfield™. To date, I now have been part of four incredibly successful co-authored books and published two books of my own.

My 'debut' as a co-author was in **Success Breakthroughs** with Jack Canfield™, author of the "Chicken Soup for the Soul" anthology books and Founder of Canfield Enterprise. My chapter is called, "Woman to Woman.".

I then joined another group to keep my balance: John Assaraf, Founder of NeuroGym™, brought me to a full cycle of awareness, as a Gestalt Theorist in my B.A. I felt I was whole once more. Finding a balance between mind, body, and soul is never an easy feat for anyone.

A year later, I had the pleasure of working with Patty Aubrey™, CEO of Canfield Enterprises and Entrepreneur. Unbeknownst to me, Patty led me down a new path of self-discovery beyond the realms of my own limitations to realize that I could still be useful in the world around me.

The long-held dream of writing a book of my own one day has now become true with **Grandma in the Box**, and now the first book of my own blessed compiled series, **Calling All Earth Angels and Healers**.

I was then taken further along into structuring a social media platform through Business in a Box (Www.Synduit.com/a/drg). I have now developed and successfully reinvented myself once more in life. They say, "third time's a charm", so, as a fledgling literary author and activist, I am meeting such amazing, encouraging people from vast backgrounds, from all around the world. Sharing the message of hope, just as others were there for me when I was unable to see out of the dark hole of despair when I fell ill, trying so hard not to believe what the doctors were telling me and my family. I overcame all the odds and obstacles with the help of many, personally and professionally and as part of an inspirational group that met my needs. I now choose to support and give back to others. With just a spark of hope and encouragement, I believe anyone can find their own true path to happiness.

This journey has helped me reinvent myself after a life-threatening situation that arose a few years ago in my life. Each experience has helped me realize not only my own potential but also the potential of me continuing to be a support to others in their time of searching. Even though my health may not allow me to do a 9-5 job, I have found my niche in life once more and I am able, through writing and speaking, to share my wealth of knowledge with the vast population of the world with the aid of modern technological tools.

Now, if you had told me ten years ago that I would be writing a book, and co-authoring with Jack and my two other esteemed colleagues and authors, Dr. Sundi Sturgeon, author of the **Warrior Women With Angel Wings** series, and Jill Rhiannon, author of **Reading Between The Signs**, I would have laughed and said my 8th-12th grade English teachers would have rolled over in their grave's laughing. But here I am, writing the preface to my second authored book with three more books to come soon.

So, I challenge each of you to keep reading great encouraging books, talk to amazing people who you admire, go to places you have always wanted to go; even if it just creating a vision board, using affirmations, or connecting with like-minded/spirited people. I always believe in applying The Law of Attraction and Universal Love of self and others doing this will create the wealth of success for your own intended goals of personal and spiritual needs.

With many blessings and with much love, make sure to,

"Have A Great Life"

DrG

About the Compiler

Geri Magee, Ph.D., is an honest, direct and assertive woman whose life's journey has helped both women and men from around the world achieve their highest potential.

She has developed herself as a businesswoman, author, public speaker, educator, therapist/executive-mentor, mediator, empathic cosmic conduit, reader and seer. She has been a great employee and loves being an independent contractor/author.

Geri has received several "Woman of the Year" awards both professionally and personally. She has a background as a p/t radio host, she has been on Good Morning America, Sacramento and in South Sound magazine. In the past few years, she has received multiple awards. Her most recent was Best Author in 2018 for a co-authored book "Success Breakthroughs", with Jack Canfield and author of "Chicken Soup for The Soul"™. In 2018 she co-authored three other "Best Selling Books" in the first week on Amazon and Kindle with Jack Canfield, Sundi Sturgeon and Jill Rhiannon

Geri started as a financial and estate planner at age twenty-three. She later made a midlife career shift after earning a master's degree in Systemic Therapy and Business Organizational Development.

Finding the balance with the financial world and the spiritual world was one of the greatest gifts she could have ever received. Her spiritual journey to date is an interesting step-by-step incline and learning process to know her higher power and the knowledge of universal love.

DrG created the "Universal Relationship Pyramid"; for over twenty-five years utilizing the theory in career market helping individuals, couples and families, or work environments and team members who begin to create a safe home or working environment. It is easy to do if you break the pyramid down brick by brick. You can create the life you want, need and deserve; firstly, by understanding who you are and secondly, how you choose to react to and resolve the various situations and environments around you.

Later in life, she finalized her Reiki Master courses while in Japan. This journey brought a stillness inside of herself and the realization that the higher power/universe is giving us healing methods that we can learn and rely on every day to create harmony within ourselves and the world around us.

Japan was a particularly memorable spiritual journey for her to experience and she longs to return there one day soon; with many other adventures planned on her life's journey. DrG found each step and turn of life's events were powered through resilience, patience, and angelic guidance. This brought her to an awareness of self-love and the important lesson of universal love for each other.

She wishes to acknowledge so many people who have selflessly helped her get to where she is in life. Geri feels the deepest gratitude to all who have been on this journey throughout her lifespan. These are the earth angels and healers who have guided her throughout her darkest hours. Her love for you is deep and she feels indebted for the blessings; and whether positive or not, they have all helped her develop into the person she is today.

She thanks all from the bottom of her heart and is sending you many blessings and much love.

A Note from the Editor

I would like to take this opportunity to thank Geri Magee (DrG) for entrusting me as the editor for this book.

Calling All Earth Angels & Healers has been a labor of love, learning, growth, and synchronicity. It has been a pleasure to read through and edit each co-author submission, each of whom has a story to tell from their own unique perspective, experience and outlook that is sure to guide, illuminate and resonate with the readers' own journey, as it has my own.

Grateful thanks go to all the co-authors' who have contributed to this life-changing compendium; without you, this book would not be possible.

It is here that I must mention recent news whilst this book is in production before publication... one of our much-loved co-authors and friend is going through some major health issues and needs our support, love and prayers. We are so thankful to have come to know Elsbeth Shields, and have been blessed by her great wisdom, knowledge, experience and understanding that she has imparted for other anthologies that I have been involved with. Please take a moment as you read these words to send your love and prayers to Elsbeth.

You can find more of Elsbeth's previous writings in Sundi Sturgeon's *Warrior Women with Angel Wings* anthology, *"Gleaning the Positive from the Negative"* and Jill Rhiannon's *Reading Between the Signs* and *Gaia Goddess: From Motherhood to Healing Mother Earth*.

Elsbeth also had plans for a book of her own and to co-author in my own upcoming anthology, *Soul Illuminations – dreams, visions & insight.* Elsbeth has given her permission to still publish in *Soul Illuminations*, which I will be doing as a tribute to her. With much love, gratitude and many blessings,

Karen Tants, November 5th, 2019

Contents

Author, Public Speaker, and Trainer on Relationships and Finance,
Concierge Therapist, Inspirational Mentor/Coach, MFT, MHC,
Theorist of "The Universal relationship Therapist." Master Reiki,
Financial and Estate Planner, Certified Senior Advisor.

Am I an Earth Angel or Healer?

By Geri Magee aka DrG

Am I an earth angel or healer? This question was commonly asked when I spoke to people who were interested in co-authoring *Calling All Earth Angels and Healers.* In fact, Earth Angels and Healers are truly no different in the intent to help and heal. The quantifying factors that define whether you are earth angel or healer are subjective of each ones' own spiritual belief system. The religious practices and belief systems that may apply the knowledge of oneself, understanding, and coming to acceptance that helps you find your calling.

I have discovered, over time, that those who believe in angelic beings and a "God", generally prefer to be called an earth angel. Whereas healers identify with their religious or non-religious beliefs that help someone to identify as a healer. By the same token, an earth angel may have similar beliefs and practices to that of a healer.

"What is an Earth Angel?" In my theory, "The Universal Relationship Pyramid", I describe Earth Angels and Healers as those who go through the gunk and muck, picking up all that is living and bringing them through the tough areas of their life. Additionally, they share in all the joys of the many and varied lives in celebration.

If you pose the question: "Well, am I an earth angel or healer?" The answer is always, "Yes!". Many asked, "How do you see me as an earth angel or healer?" My first answer is always, "You would not be talking with me unless you were a healer or earth angel." We are all guided by each other's light and love that shines a light stronger than ourselves when we are in need.

My first question was, "Tell me what interested you in co-authoring this particular book, *Calling All Earth Angels and Healers?*". Many knew what their calling was immediately. Some did not.

In either case, the reason being that no matter how and what we each think; when we lead, more are seeing how we aide others in our daily lives. Not only humans but all living things are the guiding light to our own calling. Many have a calling for plants, animals, children, the elderly, the earth and the sky, communities and global issues and concern. We all do what we need to do to sustain life.

However, our careers may not always be our calling. Your calling can also be your hobby, or varying interests of all kinds (see the definitions at the end of this book). For instance, you may work as a programmer but in your free time you work in the yard as a gardener; you are caring for the earth, your family, your home. As a nurse, you may care for people, but on weekends you are a whale rescuer; which is a great calling of the duality of both humans and nature; with both being mammals the connection is easy. When I spoke about this with someone I know, he responded that he never thought of his life in that way. It changed his perspective of life and how he contributes to the world each day, both personally and professionally.

I have received many calls asking: "Am I a healer?", yes very specific to the many different spiritual beliefs that one has, that may not be part of a religious organization and does not believe in monotheistic or multiple God/s. But they do believe in a spirit realm some said. Many others believed in the natural order of things and the healing light as well as universal love as the guidance; in which case they prefer not to follow the 'earthbound' angel thought system. Buddhism, for example, does not have hierarchy or earthly angelic beings, but they very seriously practice the art of healing in multiple ways, which brings them into a spiritual realm of belief systems.

My years of studying multiple religions as my hobby in theology (part of my education as well as the teachings influencing my belief system) brought me to experience angelic being as well as universal love and healing light for others. The elderly, children, teens, families, couples and varying systems of work environments are live entities that cause a 'chain reaction' that goes into an energetic life of its own. This does need healing if the system is not working.

For instance, a team of colleagues can be alive or dead; subject to management direction and intent, a team will either survive or break apart, the energy of which is palpable (can be felt).

The systems in our personal life are alive; the energy as a couple or a family can take on a life of its own and may need angelic light or healing. The 'couple' relationship is a whole entity of its own, as depicted in my theory, "The Universal Relationship Pyramid." http://Www.UniversalRelationship.com

Now, without a doubt, the family is a system that needs guidance daily. We need to feed our family, cloth them and check the wellbeing of each other; just like a team, the family systemically works together or does not choose to work together. In either case, it still functions as an entity of its own.

The human body is also a multifunctioning system of its own. We regulate our homeostasis state, not only physically but mentally and spiritually in one way or another based on the individual belief system. We need to care for ourselves and at some point, most of us need care as well. For instance, if you go for a haircut, you are getting a healer working on you.

We know a Barber/Hairdresser helps you change how you look, which inadvertently can change how we feel and perceive things in your daily life. Having your hair cut or styled rejuvenates you physically, mentally and in many cases, spiritually.

"How?", I was asked by a friend who is a hairdresser. My response was, "They feel better after their cut", "Why?" We both know it's physical. "Answer me this", I said to her, "How many times do people talk to you about their family, life, work...?", "All the time!", she responded. So, when they walk away, almost everyone goes away with a sense that they have been cared for and heard. I then told her, "You are a healer!" and knowing her spiritually, I told her, she is also an earth angel.

Here is where duality can be performed in an instantaneous way, without us realizing what our impact can be on someone else either good or bad without ever knowing what we just did for the person, the work we do, or the environment in which we live.

My daughter asked, "Mom you are putting Satan in your book, Aren't you?". I had not realized it, but yes, I need to, since he is an earthbound angel in monotheistic belief systems. Lucifer was an angel cast down from Heaven to rule the Earth. In scriptures, it speaks of him and his followers, not only the angelic realm but also other living beings. Humanity being the main one he focuses his attention on. Many forget how deceiving Satan can look or make things seem to be. It is written how beautiful he is and can deceive people.

We know, as humans, our impact on each other can take such a toll in a negative way. We become depleted, drained, anxious or depressed. All of these are the trickle-down effects from doing or being around something, in which the causality has such a negative impact. Now some may call it "Satan's work", and the list is long of the many adages that describe him. Many are very interesting and can be labeled whether they are human, animal or even environmental; e.g., politicians, snakes, 'the abyss', are just a few easy depictions that we as humans describe the vastness of realms that can be negatively affected.

However, there are still many who do not believe in Satan worldwide. But all believe that there is a negative impact that can cause adverse effects to someone else's energy, life, and health which causes the depletion in oneself.

As for me, there are many names I call when this negativity impacts my life; 'the work of the devil', 'negative energy' and 'karma' are just a few. My list goes on from my vast knowledge of theocratic history. I tend to pull my experiences from that suits usually the situation I am currently in.

The first step in not allowing yourself to go astray is to stay in tune with your body. What is your body telling you? Your gut, heart, and mind are all parts of your being that give the green light or show the red flag (go ahead or stop; right there!). *Listening to our bodies is an important first step in the healing process.*

For those who believe the soul lives within the body as a separate entity, the soul in these beliefs is what drives the person. In the science area of my theory, The Universal Relationship Pyramid, spirituality and science go hand in hand, but mostly in opposition to each other. Many believe we are spiritually driven, and there are those who believe scientific and mathematical equations can lead us to a higher extension of our selves; and of course, there are those who do not believe either exist. Then there are many, like me, who believe both can coexist within each other, making us whole in mind, body, and spirit.

The past few years I have been severely ill of health, this being what motivated me in writing this book. I needed to block out things, places, events, tv, and even people. As a healer and empath, I could not handle the negative impact of everything around me that went along with my illness, because it brought with it such deep unhappiness and sorrow. It was not an easy process to go through and loneliness set in from the multiple losses I had to give up in order to sustain my wellbeing.

The actions I chose during this time period caused my health to improve significantly. It was the effect of bringing only from the few resources I could receive positive energy into my life. The biggest tools I used were of my beliefs in The Laws of Attraction (multiple coauthors and inspirers). As well as Dr. Masaru Emoto's Water Crystal Theory; of how positive environments can have a significant effect on our body which is made up of water, as well as negative environments can have an ill effect on oneself as well.

Now, with my belief in Reiki by Dr. Mikao Usui along with the multiple people that brought in pure light and love into my life at that point in one form or another. This belief helped me heal to a point that I can feel useful once more like an earth angel and healer to myself and others.

When a healer falls ill the best form of healing would be to go into nature, take a walk in the park, put yourself around children, call upon positive friends or go to positive environments that suit your need/s. Allow yourself to enjoy the moment you are in and vitality sets in, in some form or another. Finding the balance is never easy to do it is all about the journey anyway. "Isn't it?"

As earthbound angels and healers, we are given gifts throughout life that we must recognize in order to experience fulfillment in oneself and the environment around us. That was the key to my turning point, for me to come back once more in order to reinvent myself with the help of numerous earth angels and healers worldwide. My thanks to each and every one of you for enriching me and coming into my basement of gunk to take me to the light once more. Many blessings with love and gratitude.

Earth Angels and Healers of all Kinds

I trust this will be a resourceful guide in your search for belonging in this vast universe. Earth Angels and Healers overlap in so many ways. Thus, I decided to keep the definitions together so you may find yourself amongst the many masses of people who flock to their profession due to their soul's desire and to their heart's content. Examples (not limited to):

Actor, Aged care worker, Alternative therapist e.g., Bowen and Homeopathy, Ambulance driver/Medic, Animals, Assistant, Author, Baker, Banker, Barber, Barperson, Beggar, Boxer, Builder, Cleaner, Clerk, Coach, Comedian, Computer guru, Coroner, Counselor, Cuisine/food/chef, Dentist, Designer, Disability Support Worker, Doctor, Dreamer, Editor,

Electrician, Empath, Energy worker, Engineer, Executive, Fae, Firefighter, Florist, Forward-thinker, Garbage Collector, Government Employee, Hairdresser, Hospitality worker, Hotel Manager, Housewife, Idealist, Inventor, Illustrator, Jockey, Judge, King, Lawyer, Lightworker, Manufacturer, Marketer, Mediator, Medium, Mentor, Midwife, Minister, Monk, Musician, Nature, Newsreader, Nun, Nurse, Official, Oracle/tarot reader, Pastor, Philosopher, Photographer, Playwright, Plumber, Politician, Publisher, Preacher, Priest, Prince, Princess, Property developer, Prophet, Public Speaker, Purchaser, Queen, Reiki I – Healing Self, Reiki II – Healing of others, Reiki III – Master Level, Sailor, Saint, Seer, Shaman, Shapeshifter, Social media guru, Sound Healer,

Spiritual guru, Surgeon, Undertaker, Vet, Volunteer, Weightlifter, White Lighter, Writer, Yoga teacher, Yogi/Yogini.

You may not see your Calling amongst the list here; nonetheless, you are still an Earth Angel or Healer at/in somewhere in your life with someone, or something, around that you care for.

If interested in sharing your calling, please contact DrG so you can be part of what we all hope will be a series of books featuring peoples who have a love for their "Calling" and want to share it with the world for the inspiration and betterment of all.

The Healer Within (Wisdom Mastery)

By Elsbeth Shields

Wisdom mastery is about looking within and remembering that your wisdom resides in every cell of your body. It is nothing that is taught to you; you have only to remember yourself. You carry the answers to the questions you ask. *You* are the gift you have been seeking. Your internal guides bring awareness within your cellular structure, enabling the internal sounds of your nervous system to "vibrate" matter into an understanding of its nature and structure for remembering all the parts of yourself. *(That's what 'invoking' is all about.*

It's a tool to help you remember your Divinity and tune into your intuition or your third eye; turning that 'eye' within and looking for your guides in your spinal column).

You can read, be taught by others, and emulate as many people you honor outside of your Self; the jewel is found when you choose to realize and 're-cognize' that your cells carry every piece of the Divine within your physical structure. It is then that you awaken to become the tremendous "healer" (aka facilitator, guide, coach, shaman, priest, etc.) that you came here to be. Perhaps offering transformational healing to your clients may be a more appropriate approach. That is when you share what you understand through *empowering* others; not to "heal" others. Calling oneself a 'healer' has become a "hype" word that disempowers others who depend on looking outside of themselves. We are ALL healers. There is no separation between being a healer and a receiver. We are all One. We must stop duality thinking and recognize it when we see and feel it. We are here to help others find the key that opens to their own treasure within. Then, if you must, calling yourself a healer (by definition) is more appropriate.

In the 'old days' of the sixties, seventies, and eighties, we called ourselves the 'giver' and the client the 'receiver'. We also used 'facilitator', 'coach', shaman or assistant.' Who does the real healing? If the receiver is not yet ready to heal, no healing will happen. It will just be a good or bad, short-lived experience. It all depends on how much inner awareness *(or receptor sites in the brain)* has occurred within the receiver.

The first time the recipient has a moment of distrust or the recurring of the same unhealed thoughtforms that created the dis-ease in the first place, the symptom will re-create itself. I've learned that if a client would rather "not" heal, they won't. If the receiver wants healing, he or she will display the willingness to open to healing energy and allow the reception of such energy. A trusting relationship begins between the giver and receiver to spark the flow of energy. The energy I speak of is called, "Love." Anything, unlike love, carries some type of fear. If you are not experiencing your own centeredness when sharing space with your client, you are not in harmony.

Each of us must be dedicated to our own healing; it's not about going to a healer with the responsibility on the healer to fix something; there is nothing to be fixed. Each person is on his or her own path. It is not your task as a healer to heal anyone, as each will awaken in their own time, and maybe not even in this lifetime. It *is* your task to heal yourself fully, and then be available to help others find their own availability within to heal themselves.

Awareness begins with you. Start now to heal yourself. Most of you reading this chapter have already done deep soul-searching. I have witnessed wonderfully aware people like you in the spiritual avenues of 'healing' and still frequently observe the façade of many shades of fear-based projections, attitudes, position, judgments, beliefs and illusions running deeply beneath subconscious states-of-being through gossip, jealousies, and other projections placed upon other healers or clients, etc. Your personal life may be less in harmony than what you put out to the world. *(If you are skilled and centered in the avenues of healing modalities, then you can choose to step aside from your personal world, and enter the spirit world which incorporates 'wholeness' and perform the 'healing' from that place within the true 'you' that resides in your heart-mind).*

It's not about the 'you' that makes up your personality, saying, "I'm better than you", thus creating separation; it's about coming from your heart's loving awareness that says, "I love this beautiful soul who has come to share life's trauma and lessons with me. I am honored to be part of his/her journey into Oneness." That's why I offer "Transformational Healing Services" rather than calling myself a healer.

I learned thirty years ago that my (and your) soul energy has nine aspects of Self which include your "Center."

These aspects are:

1) Physical Body

2) Heart energy

3) Ability to form Personal Relationships which include Cosmic Union with our Source

4) High Self Awareness

5) Clear Mind (as well as the Trickster that pops up when we are not in harmony)

6) Dreaming Body

7) Soul Mind

8) Personality

9) Center, Above and Below which is our Vital Force Energy.

Is there any reason why I also say that each of us has our own individual healing to do in order to be in total harmony with all aspects of "Self" and others to help create a peaceful and unified world? It will be only when mass consciousness reaches that still place within the Center that is everywhere in all beings. There will be those who disagree with what *"is"* or *"will be"* possible for us to lovingly understand with compassion the life-views of others. It means opening our hearts. It's not necessary to have the same beliefs as beliefs come from fear in one's mind about 'doing the right thing.' We really want to live in our hearts in 'harmonic convergence' with each other. We can develop trust toward obtaining peaceful spaces once we master stepping out of victim consciousness of judgments, conditional thinking, and beliefs that keep us trapped in a cage, looking out only as far as we can stick our head past the bars which are basically just past our nose! We miss a whole lot of possibilities and miracles that are tucked around the edges surrounding that cage that can become visible when the door opens to free us from our mind's programming.

My spiritual master *(who ascended in 1998)* was a star visitor whose birth was prophesized years before she was born, *(known as a 'virgin birth'; of which there are many such beings on the planet even now. Her mother was human; her father a star being).* Her Hungarian teacher carried my teacher's birth chart for over 40 years before she found my teacher who was the holder of the whispered tradition lineage called "Mehuna" that was passed from teacher to student for thousands of years. She was profoundly the most intelligent woman I had ever met! She was of self-sovereign consciousness, and not of this world. She came in with the teachings in her consciousness, was raised in seclusion to remember and retain the teachings, and in the 1980s, she began the search for the teachers who could bring the teaching forward. Her soul was ancient. Her work facilitated the realization of the untapped human potential in all of us and addressed the enormous challenge of alleviating suffering for all beings. I gathered with her and fifty other initiates and began the wildest ride into the 'art of living' that I've ever experienced. As a result, I became an ordained Akhutiu lightworker priest and master shaman of the pre-dynastic ancient Egyptian Mehuna mysteries after six years of study with my master teacher. (*The teachings start at 9,000 or 10,000 B.C. going all the way back into pre-history to 250,000 BC and going back further hundreds of thousands of years, all of which were inhabited by star beings*).

She opened secret seals that had never been opened before for 10,000 years, and higher truths rang out around the earth. As a united group of individuals, we created the intention to awaken the masses through our breath and internal sounds. We joined thousands of others stationed throughout the world to participate in the awakening of humanity. During the 1980s others began to awaken because the 'basin of attraction' had been set to "*surge ahead*" during the Harmonic Convergence. Protected ancient knowledge began to surface. The secrets went into the 'mindstream' (nervous system) of each initiate who self-actualized not only within themselves; but also sparked remembrance in others. Even while sleeping, we kept an invisible tape, spinning miracles in our brain, chanting the sounds carrying peace and forgiveness throughout ourselves and the universe.

I hardly ever slept. When we finished for the day, she would say, "Chant this word 10,000 times before awakening in the a.m." We performed these requests with honor and gratitude. I learned lucid dreaming so I could walk between the worlds during my dream state and became a Djeddu Speaker - that of being able to decipher what my dreams were telling me and to communicate with others also in the dream-state.

The many conscious beings on the planet are now experiencing what we were being taught thirty years ago. Our universal 'third eye' has begun to awaken to our mastery within and without. It only takes you (and I) maintaining a state of loving-kindness, with no positional or attitudinal thinking, or projections attached; just pure love to heal our world containing a population of seven billion or more diverse individuals. To see others as 'right and wrong' is a second chakra unhealed problem that is within you. Please heal yourself; then you can help to educate and empower the world's suffering people. It is time to join in "Cosmic Union" with your Source that lives within your second chakra (pelvic zone) through the waters of compassionate understanding. Please stop participating in warlike thinking which creates separation.

My essence is that of a shaman. This is a little different than a 'healer.' The shaman is balanced in both male and female attributes, is able to walk between the worlds, to see/feel/integrate the unseen and describe to you what hasn't 'appeared' yet to your awareness in the hopes that your receptor sights will begin connecting within your brain that which you already know and have forgotten.   I chose the avenues of action, word, sound, and breath to share what I have come to know within.

For me, it encompasses the ability to trust the universal energy of "God" *(or whatever name you wish to call it)* and know that God also lives in my heart. Once I consciously allow my soul mind (and ego) to live within my heart, I surrender myself to my process of unfolding my life's passion, which is to help you continue your own path without suffering. *[I trust that you already know much of how to be aware of your heart's energy. I empower you to follow your path which forges the way to your heart. I also teach you the keys that allow you to consciously stay in the presence of your heart awareness.]*   You have the capacity to heal yourself. Faith is a developed emotion. Cultivate faith in yourself, now and always. You are doing God's work through your own God-Self.

You must build upon the foundation of your wisdom mastery as you strive to become a true healer with no ulterior motives.   Many of you are now integrating Low Self (subconscious), Middle Self (conscious mind) and High Self (Superconscious God Self) toward the goal of living more fully each moment "merging with any state safely, skillfully, and at choice." Wisdom is the ability to walk in equilibrium, balance, poise and without judgment knowing that your High, Middle and Low Selves are fully balanced and in the present time. It's being able to know without thinking, to look, listen, hear, taste and act from within, trusting yourself, listening to your cells talk to each other, receiving messages of long-forgotten knowledge of thousands of years ago--- all inside your body. It's about knowing that you are connected to everything there is, was, and ever shall be. And it's about living in your heart, with your flame burning brightly for all to experience, so they may come and drink from the waters that flow from your heart-stream for nourishment and healing.

I met my teachers at age forty--- a lot older than most of you reading this chapter.

(I am now 76 and the 'alive and joyous' woman you see on the front page of this chapter was only two months ago!) While studying in the mysteries, I was on a 'jet plane of awareness' intent on catching up with my personal growth that I had missed out on due to being married young and following my husband's desires; being denied my own, even when I spoke up. I 'caught up' from where I left off in other lifetimes to bring forth the person I am now. I discovered that my mind was "thinking" and "feeling" within the structure of my physical body. I learned that there is a "mind in each cell." I began the feat of communicating with my cellular structure. I would feel an impulse or a tone playing in my head *and* listen to the orchestra playing in my cells. The sounds started physically shifting me. Vibrations would flood through different parts of me and my cellular structure would shift. I knew something wonderful was happening within me. *(It was just a matter of time before I met my next husband in 1982 and enjoy true happiness and equality. His love enabled me to attend the mystery schools while he "fathered" my growing children. We were together for thirty years until he passed in 2012).*

I am self-created, and so are you, moment by moment; dying each moment and welcoming the next.

In that same vein, I suspect highly that many of you reading this also carry what I call 'compassionate understanding' within. If so, you also carry untiring unconditional love for all suffering on the planet.

I asked myself in 1976 when my first divorce was finalized, "Why not walk each moment being present in the NOW?" I was talking on the phone, and suddenly the phone disconnected and started beeping a busy tone Di, Di, Di, Di, Di. I was receiving a 'transmission' that spoke loudly to my heart. I thought, *This is the sound of Present Time! It is passing me by, while I wallow in pain and suffering. Every second I spend in suffering; I am erasing the joy I could be experiencing now. I'm hearing my life pass me by. I have been wasting my 'time' trying to hold onto something that is not benefiting either of us."* I sat there listening to the sound of 'Now' coming into my ears. I heard "Di" go into the past for several minutes with sadness; then turned it around and welcomed the incoming "Di."

It was a synchronistic awakening for me with the phone telling me to stay in the present time and stop taking shortcuts through the thickets of pain and suffering in my private life that was causing me horrendous strife and unhappiness.

I asked myself:

"How many more lessons do you need to learn, Elsbeth? What better time than NOW to honor everything that has brought you to the place you are NOW, which is a seeker, embracing love more deeply than ever because you are seeking peace, happiness, and unity for both yourself and all living sentient beings. You must stop separating yourself from what you already know even if you found yourself 'used and abused

emotionally and mentally'. It lies within your knowingness, not in books or other's actions. "

I have to say that what came next was the impulse to go over to the library in our home which held hundreds of books. I systematically pushed them off the shelves onto the floor in an outward display of what the striving to "be good enough" had caused in both our lives. Already more aware of my heart energy at the time, there was nothing I could do to save my marriage. I realized I must let go of everything outside myself and listen for the first time within myself for answers. [When I attended the Mystery Schools, I learned that the ancient word for "NOW" was "DI". My inner knowingness had remembered the word through the synchronicity of my experiences in the moment thirteen years before! This is an example of how we remember what we've forgotten.]

In truth, because you are reading this chapter, your True and Authentic Self already acknowledges that you are also an enquirer who is seeking ways to enable yourself to look and listen within, deeply enough to hear your cells speaking to you. Life is an exciting and challenging catalyst for change. You can make or break your Self into a thousand pieces, tear yourself apart with your pain, destroy your Self with thoughts of anger, hatred, blame, and stubbornness, and dis-own your Self even further by creating sickness and perish from this earth as an escape from life. Or, you can break out of your old patterns and birth your Self anew, choosing to LIVE for the first time in your life! It's never too late! We are healers because we are choosing life.

Each of you (healer or not) has a precious treasure to offer the world that is buried deep within your cellular structure. It is now your challenge in this current lifetime to discover the treasure that was birthed within you when you decided to arrive here on this beautiful planet. You chose to come here, by way of choosing the place, date, time, and parents to be born into. There are no mistakes. You are a divine being and it was divinely written in the cosmos that you would be part of the awakening you are experiencing today *before* you were born. You came with a purpose. You forgot about it. Are you living it yet? Have you remembered yourself yet? Do you feel goosebumps? Always, feel yourself within and ask, seek, and feel your cells respond. Learn to "read your Self" in ways you thought impossible before.

Claim now the truth within you. You ARE lovable, and you ARE good enough. Start smiling at everyone, even if they resist your smile. Start small and grow your smile. Everyone knows a true smile and will return the gesture. You will begin to feel good and your muscles will shift into a *real* smile. It brings the light in your heart up to your mouth, bursting out from your heart's awareness. You can't frown when you are happy, can you? Remember always that happiness births from within you.

Start unpacking now: Your judgments, blame, traits, fears, personal edicts, self- serving obsessions, projections, opinions, and attitudes. You speak truth from your High Self when your heart allows your mind (with all its sabotaging tendencies) to transform within your heart where it can learn a better way to serve you.

Your heart is so full of love, forgiveness, healing powers, and spirit aliveness that erases pain and suffering. Heal yourself. Your primary focus can then be aimed toward empowering and healing others, as a healer, shaman, guide, friend, facilitator, coach, brother, sister, Mom or Dad, etc.).

It is said that one moment of judgment, blame, or condemnation creates 10,000 lifetimes of Karma, but only one moment of compassionate understanding will erase all Karma. Whew! What a relief that one is! Your choice can be easy and delightful!

You are such a powerful aspect of Universal Energy; all that is needed is your breath of awareness. Your breath *is* Life. *(Sound and breath combined create, light, which shines Love throughout the universe and can be focused thousands of miles away, creating infinite healing energy from your body's wisdom which guides you from within).*

There is no need for "savior consciousness": We don't have to go out and 'save the world.' You have already been graced by the Divine. Each person can now become capable of being at the absolute center, sending messages from that place rather than from our programming. We will be united throughout the world *when and if* we remember it all starts from within us and flows out from our loving heart which is connected to the Source. Let go of 'should and ought'. Look within, for the healer within you will speak to your knowledge and grant you the capabilities of being and living in the present time with love, joy, bliss, truth, freedom, and unity with all there is, was and ever shall be. May you be blessed always, in all ways.

The lesson for today and always: Speaking absolute truth (your Godself Spirit embodied from above, living in your heart) will set you free for you are already graced. You need do nothing more than just "BE" yourself in your loving and compassionate heart which knows only love. Amen.

Amen explained: In the ancient language before Sanskrit, vibrational sounds came out of one's nervous system. Our body's cells remember such vibrational sounds over many lifetimes. Whole philosophies are then created in one word. The word "Amen" is translated in three syllables: "A" means truth or I. "AM" means grace. "MEN" means eternally (or forever). This sound means, *"I am graced in truth eternally.* Believe it, remember it, and live it fully. It is your divine connection to your Source which guides you when you listen within. That Source is with you always when you breathe, live and speak from your mind that lives in your heart. It has nothing to do with religion (beliefs). It has a whole lot to do with your spiritual connection to your own Divine Source, God, Creator, and Great Spirit. May you all be blessed with this truth.

Biography - Elsbeth Shields (aka Sia MutSahu)

With over 50 years of training and private practice, Elsbeth (Sia MutSahu) is an accomplished, captivating speaker, Pre-Dynastic Egyptian Shaman, and Akhutiu Light-worker Priest whose teaching brings about healing and evolutionary consciousness to her students and clients. In addition, she offers naturopathic techniques and life coaching combined with Kalos Ten Priority

Healing, Reiki, EFT, Pain Management, Meditation, Bodywork/Massage, Organ Balancing, Cranio-Sacral Therapy, and Energy Balancing.

She is deeply devoted to serving others both privately and in seminars. She has dedicated her life to the evolution of love in the world, both on a personal and a planetary level. She is intuitive; guiding her students toward hope and possibilities. She teaches that the sense of liberation into our full potential begins to open when we face our illusions and our personal truths which are rooted in our unhealed subconscious mind. Healing happens when understanding an event or person with compassion brings forgiveness and a loving heart.

She also reminds us that we are never separate from our Divine Essence (God, Supreme Being, Great Spirit, Creator etc.) The answers lay within us when we open the channel that leads us to the flame that is burning brightly in our hearts and connects with our Divine Source. Using Breath and Sound practices, heart/soul awareness becomes radiant for all to see and feel while creating a safe place for you to strive to be a better version of YOU.

Her teaching focuses on the mysteries of 9000 to 250,000 BC, (during the star being era) when the Divine Feminine was recognized as well as the Divine Father. She travels the circuit of the Bay Area, Yuba, Sutter, Butte, and Sacramento Counties for those who wish to continue their evolutionary growth into 5th dimensional awareness by remembering their radiance within, using breath, sound, and self-actualization to help create freedom, aliveness, joy, and bliss for all.

If you wish to host a seminar in your own home or make an appointment for a private session, please call for information by contacting her at elsbeshields@aol.com (without the 'th'). Mobile: 1-530-632-6489 (Text) Land Phone: Office:1-530-755-2146 Message

Blue Fire Forming

By Laverne E. Denyer

A Short Story: The true story of a young girl and her quest for understanding of spiritual and metaphysical topics. The young girl is me, so this is my story between the ages of 5 and 20. I fought the battle to be understood and to understand why I saw the world so differently from everyone around me. I met the challenge of discovery on my own with no mentor, except the spiritual beings who came in to support me. The influence that the force of God and my spirit helpers has had on my life is inspiring to me. I hope you will enjoy it as well.

At five, she has already established her place in the world. When not climbing trees and roofs, she is making friends with other people's pets and livestock.

Her parents attempt to guide her, but this free spirit is already listening to a different drummer. Where did she come from? What makes her different? The difference is that she has been called to earth once more as a leader, healer, and role model.

She is a child of the blue flame. Her life begins with the flame; with blue fire swirling, flowing. The God-force gathers itself to animate a small lump of clay, a girl-child. God sends forth a beacon of power burning bright. The newly created personality survives and grows.

The girl-child is active and adventurous. She is mischief incarnate. The remembered knowledge of other earthly visits is reflected in her eyes. Strange expressions cross her face, expressions of wisdom unusual for a child. The wisdom... the awareness... is disconcerting. They watch her with a discerning eye.

The adults in her life are mystified. Just what is it about this effervescent bundle of energy that captivates and frightens? Is it the fact that she seems to know so much more than a child of five? Or is it that she is always there when something unusual happens? What is it?

Rarely stationary, generally noisy, always inquisitive and down-right stubborn; she is already an enigma. What does the future hold for her? What about the people around her?

Already, she is a neighborhood leader. Other children are attracted to her like metal filings to the magnet. She settles disputes and plans new adventures. Like the time they went on an early morning raid of the prune orchard and Mr. Wellerman fired a load of rock salt at Timmy. But since she had heard in her mind when it was time to go, they escaped his anger and his recognition. The adults are perplexed. How can a child of five command such authority over eight and twelve-year-old children? The mystery continues.

At eight, she explains psychic experiences to friends and relatives. They think she is strange and try to ignore her stories. She keeps on sharing and they shake their heads in concern.

She tells of conversations with spirits. The adults don't know that she truly does talk to spirits, regularly. They don't believe. She tells of her invisible friend Laurelei. They ignore her. What a shame.

She talks about pretty colors around their bodies; and they don't understand. They don't know about an aura, and she doesn't know the name yet.

She talks about flying through the sky and watching her friends crawl upon the ground. Little do they know that astral travel is common to her. Her spirit freely leaves her body to soar through the sky. They laugh. But they wonder.

She seems to just "know" what will happen next... taking changes in stride. They worry.

She talks of spirit battles and of good and evil in another world. They cross themselves.

Such tales are unnerving. To reduce their anxiety, the adults begin to tell her she has an over-active imagination and needs to stop "making things up." After all, stories about travel through Heaven and Hell MUST be fabrications. Talking to Great-Great Grandmother? Absurd! Where does she get such ideas?

Sadly, she believes her elders. Her direct link with God and the Angels shuts down. She loses touch with the blue flame. She becomes earthbound and "normal."

Life as a normal child isn't as exciting or wonderful as it was before. A least it brings acceptance, even friendship. When you are nine, being "just like everyone else" is important and necessary. She lives her life *their* way and feels empty inside. She isolates herself from the unknown. She buries the flame, and her true spirit rests.

The inner dark times begin. The blue light of awareness is dimmed. There is no contact with the higher realms. There are no exciting astral adventures. There are no invisible visitors. She is alone and lonely. It is lonely in the "real" world when you know about God's place. She shuts down for the sake of other people and their friendship. Yet she feels alone. Earthly friendships are not enough. She stays alone in the dark for two years. She cries inside.

Then, at eleven, she knows something is missing. She feels so empty. She simply cannot be content. Her buried heart stirs to awaken. She knows there is more to life. She rethinks her decision to accept other people's opinions. Maybe there is something they are missing. She decides to release the bonds she placed on the blue flame and renews her link with the unknown.

The decision is made. She opens her mind to secret thoughts carefully ignored for so long. She lets her senses wander in uncharted realms as she reawakens her spiritual being. She turns up the light and again rides the power of the magic flame. Her spirit breaks free of earthly limits.

Once again, she practices astral travel. She rides the blue flame; her spirit is free. Trips to adjoining cities are not enough. Every night, she sets her inner mind to travel to new locations in other countries. She travels the globe from New Guinea to New Zealand, learning more and more about geography and new societies.

As verification, she visits the library each following day to research the locations just visited. It is amazing how much she learns each night. Her accuracy astounds and encourages her. She is filled with wonder and excitement. It helps her geography grades in school, too.

The next step is taking along a witness or two. Of course she doesn't discuss the adventure while the witnesses are awake. But when they are sleeping, she drops by, offering an invitation to visit London, Matzatlan, Sudan or Istanbul. The travelers explore and learn. Then she takes her friend or friends home and rejoins her own body.

The test comes the next day. Waiting, she anxiously anticipates mention of the adventure. Usually, the latest traveler mentions the strange dream just experienced. It seems Michael dreamt of flying to England; and our girl-child was there as well. It felt so real! How could that be? The girl just smiles and says *"Oh? How odd."* She smiles inside. She knows that her memory is true.

By thirteen, she has rediscovered the beauty of the spiritual realm. She learns that the study of sciences other than physical is called Metaphysics. Since she has no physical mentors, she must rely on books, experiences and her inner guidance. Her curiosity and tenacity are astounding. Her personal storehouse of information and experiences is always growing.

At fifteen, she begins to share her knowledge with other individuals. Some laugh and deride her illusions. Some say she will be damned for her sacrilege. Some are simply mystified... again.

However, there are those who listen attentively, who begin to understand. Some can even share new information with her. She recounts her personal experience with the blue flame. They talk of conversations with spirits and unexplained knowledge. She finds fellow travelers, also questing for knowledge. They learn and play together.

By seventeen she shares her knowledge freely and ignores those who laugh or call her devil. She understands. She forgives.

By eighteen she understands her quest. Her path will not take her over well-trod highways. The drummer she hears beats a different rhythm than most. She recognizes the beacon of love and knowledge lighting her path. She is content.

At twenty she is introduced to her first spiritual guide. It is her father. Although he died two years prior, he decided to accept the task of helping her understand higher truths. He speaks words in her mind. He is a comfort. She will have many other guides later, spirits like Enoch, Maurice and Pteledia. How wonderful that her first tutor is a loved one she knew so well. His sense of humor helps her learn perspective. It is fun, but he makes certain she learns much.

As she travels her adult years, this woman-child of the universe tightens her bond with the alternate reality, which is the spiritual realm. She begins to share her intuitive ability freely with others. She allows the world to see her for what she is, a psychic explorer. When they laugh, she smiles. When they condemn, she forgives.

Her natural healing abilities develop. She learns how to help others create healthy bodies, minds and spirits. The power flows through her body. The fire burns through her hands, gently touching others. The more she does, the more she learns.

She seeks further knowledge. She becomes strong.

There comes a time when she is grateful for her knowledge.

While helping a client, she encounters the face of a demonic force. She meets Bast, goddess of the underworld. She MUST help the soul that is crying out to her. The help is not physical. The help is psychic. And it is dangerous.

Yet the strength of love is stronger! The God force stands as a pillar amidst the demonic force. She gathers the force of the blue flame. She shields herself with white light and the battle begins...

As the battle ends, the woman is untouched, her protection is strong. The Demon is banished! Divine order is restored.

The woman-priest is content. She has faced the challenge and done well. She knows it is not her last battle, but it was important. It was a major turning point from seeker to teacher. It taught her much.

Now she makes daily contact with the source of love, God. She continues her quest. She is a worker and traveler and minister in his light. The power is not of her—but channeled through her. She is one with it.

The Blue Fire is still forming.

Biography - Laverne E. Denyer

Born into a world different from everyone around me, I have had many experiences far beyond the norm. My soul calling is to be a Warrior Priest. I work to help people build healthy lives and follow their soul's purpose through a variety of modalities. At the same time, I am a protector and guardian of the planet and its inhabitants. All of this while living a life as a wife, a mom, and many other roles in the mundane world.

My world is filled with sights, sounds, scents, sensations, feelings and thoughts that are different from those of most people. My spiritual world leads me through many experiences. I research and practice an eclectic form of therapeutic body work. It is an important part of my life and my being. I have discovered many new (or remembered?) bits of information about ways in which we live in this world. My studies about the Living Energy System, Reincarnation, Other Life Explorations, Meditation, and other spiritual modalities play large roles in my life.

An inner drive to create a clearer, deeper connection with my spiritual self has driven me as long as I can remember. I have four published books of my own and now have been a contributing author to six others, with a contract for yet another of my own.

In my time on this planet, in this incarnation, I have had opportunities for a wide variety of experiences. They have all been important and rewarding. I wouldn't be who I am today, after all, without them. As for where I'm going, you can bet that "I ain't done yet!" I keep wondering who/what I will be tomorrow, and the day after that

In the mundane world, I have a B.A. with majors in Psychology and Religious studies, and a minor in Philosophy. Prior to that, I earned an A.S. in Architectural Design, and have designed many homes and business structures, mostly across the state of California. I also have an M.A. in Curriculum and Instruction focused on Educational Technology, and a Tier I Educational Leadership degree and credential. On top of that, I have a religious PhD in Religious Studies and Psychological Counseling. Learning and applying what is learned through all modalities is the continual pattern of my life.

The Energy of Love's Transformation

By Karen Tants

W hat (*or who*) provides food for the soul, brings music to the ears, peace to the mind and joy to the heart? As we all know, nature's food provides fuel for the body. Conversely, spiritual sustenance is provided by the unseen force beyond that which we can physically see (*which affects how we feel, our ability and desire to create, to know and to understand*), and is the driving force behind our creative power to continue existing and continuing forward on our chosen path.

Writers, artists, musicians, creative geniuses who live their passion are people who bring forth food for the soul to assist not only oneself but also others.

It requires a necessary solitude (*'soul-itude'*) to bring through what is needed at that moment in order to inspire others. The quiet, still voice that brings through the quintessential "essence" of what is necessary for a *meeting of the mind, heart and soul* to recognize, resonate with and realize our divine nature.

It is the perfect medium through which one can manifest inner Earth Angel Healer inherent within all beings as conscious, aware, intelligent Life Force. "Presence" 'comes through', activated by our intent to act as Healer or Earth Angel. It is simply "being" (*from highest intent to do good*), and feeling, thinking, intending, acting, doing *from* that beingness.

Thus, "awakened" within our sleeping form, we find ourselves Loving Unconditionally not just our own 'little self', but All-Inclusive Love, encompassing the earth and the heavens (*and earthly and heavenly beings*) with the highest intent for benevolence; harming none. It begins with the Self: self-respect and healthy boundaries, honesty, authenticity, and *living one's truth*. This act of self-love is self-healing and combined with the desire to be a better person, marks the beginning of the re-birth of the earth angel – healer. *One cannot truly love another until one love's oneself first and understands one's own connection with the life-giving force within all of creation.*

In Divine alchemy *(where one purifies the body as "The Alchemist"),* Red and White hold deep significance.

Some colors in the "palette of life" do not mix well and if combined, create chaos. Think in terms of the chakras and interactions with others; if certain colors are blended together, the result can be dull, murky and lackluster (*products of ignorance*); pretty much like relationships and situations when we don't employ our higher faculties and the higher awareness and gifts (*the ability to reason and forgive, accompanied by truth, compassion, wisdom and unconditional love)* from source.

However, Red (*when purified, Sun, King*) blended with White (*with purity of thought, Moon, Queen*) results in Pink (*Unconditional and Self-Love*).

The color vibration in the physical spectrum (rainbow) ranges in frequency from the lowest, red, to the highest, violet (in the physical realm of awareness). Of course, there are many other magnificent color frequencies of sound, light and vibratory expressions in the inner dimensions of consciousness as we expand into the heavenly realms inhabited by angelic, divine forces.

The visual appearance of pink in healing, in meditation, and/or in the aura, is a sign of self-love, unconditional all-encompassing love, benevolence, intelligent wisdom and compassion for self and others = **Mahayana**[1]. Thus, it is fair to say that Healer and Earth Angel both offer the capacity to embody the presence of the enlightened beings of Mahayana (*e.g., Quan Yin, Lady Nada, Mother Mary*): Divine Feminine.

---

[1] *Mahayana, "the great vehicle", is the great compassion that is an inherent component of enlightenment manifest in bodhisattvas (enlightenment beings); these beings postpone nirvana (final enlightenment) in order to assist and guide those beings still suffering in the cycle of rebirths. They employ what the Mahayana call "skillful means," which is the ability to know the mental and emotional capacity of the individual, and to deliver guidance appropriate to those capacities.* **https://www.patheos.com/library/mahayana-buddhism**

Earth angel brings Light to others, helps those in need, is often in the right place at the right time in order to help and assist, acts positively to uplift others or provide sanctuary for others. It can be as little as a smile to a stranger or being 'present' with someone, or of great import to prevent disaster. Sometimes, just being in the presence of earth angel can be life-changing, and many times one can be blissfully unaware of another's impact on one's life! How would you know? How could you imagine what might have occurred negatively but didn't realize because it didn't happen!

We all hold onto thoughts as we go about our day. Thoughts (*positive and negative*) affect outcomes - not only for our self but also in the lives of others. When we hold positive thoughts toward others, when we bless them and wish them the best and highest intent for happiness and love, there is no limit to the number of lives that can be transformed by our own act and influence. We can even transmute family karma and put an end to cycles of abuse! Think of thoughts as dropping little pebbles in a pond and see how far those ripples go. Think of all the creative expressions previously mentioned and see how what we create affects the whole and reverberates (*echoes*) throughout the entirety of creation.

Earth angel acts in the capacity of a healer, and Healer acts in the capacity of an earth angel. Both "hold space" with the highest intent to bring awareness of others' own inner healer/earth angel.

Physical life and its many learning paths often act as a catalyst for inner growth and expansion, and when we "arrive" at that crossroads because of an untenable situation or question our path that we no longer feel is right for us, we seek inward, searching for the truth. And when we find that truth, we are in a better position to be true toward others. We begin to unravel (*or untangle*) the 'webs of deceit' and right wrongs - thus, transmuting and transforming lives for the better on an infinite level (both known and unknown, aware and unaware) beyond time.

Ernest Hemingway coined the phrase, "courage is grace under pressure." Meaning: Even though nervous, irritated or flustered, having the courage to gracefully hold onto composure with elegance and beauty of form, manner, motion, or action.

Courage is needed as one is called to forge a new path along the unpopular, sometimes lonely 'road less traveled' on the inner journey to enlightenment and the unfoldment into one's own soul truth. Along this journey I wish you much love and many blessings on your path to revealing the purity of your own divine essence to create earth angel/healer into your life experience, empowering your creative potential.

Healing with the Angelic Realms

The "angelics" are non-physical light beings who radiate love; they do not recognize illness and disease because they see through what is not real. They see through the illusion of separation to the heart of who we are. Their love is unconditional, impersonal, and omnipresent. Angels emit a beautiful pure-white radiance that some people see with their physical eyes. These 'angel lights' look like sparkling shimmers or flashes of brightness like a flash from a camera, and sometimes these flashes can be seen while sleeping, you may suddenly be awoken by a flash in your dream. Take this as a sign that the angels are close by.

In truth, nothing and no one needs healing. All healers do is act as a channel (Divine Instrument) for Source Love energy to flow through reminding the recipient of their own healing capacity, and healing is only evident if the recipient wills it at the Soul level. The healing path is about living life from the truth, love, and a desire for change and transformation. Everyone has the capacity to be healed, simply by being. It doesn't matter where you come from, or what you have done in the past, the angels only see perfection. All else is an illusion of the mind. Here is an exercise for you to try, some of you reading this will already work in the healing area but it doesn't matter if you have not had any healing experience. Get a feel for your own energy by rubbing your hands together in circles and feel the energy between your hands as you move them close and then apart. It will feel as if there is a pressure between your hands as the energy builds up. There are chakra centers in the palms of your hands and rubbing your hands together activates and sends energy through them. If you can't feel anything just know that it is happening, and in time your sensitivity to your energy field will increase.

You may see a hazy mist, like heat haze, and even flashes of color as your energy field pulses around your body.

Sending a Chi (energy healing) **Ball to a loved one:**

Sit comfortably, preferably somewhere peaceful and quiet. Call on the angels to surround your space with love and light while you work.

Ground your energy into mother earth by visualizing tree roots growing from your feet into the earth, then send your energy back up through your crown, visualize yourself as a circuit sending your energy up and down 3 x times in a continuous flow.

Have a clear intention of who you want to send the ball to, cup your hands with your palms up, at chest level. Visualize, feel or sense the energy building through your hands, and growing larger. Blow healing into the ball, blow colors, angels, love, and light, anything else you feel you want to add to it. Feel it expand like a huge balloon, and as it grows, call on Archangel Michael and Archangel Raphael to take the chi ball from you. Visualize handing it over to them for safekeeping until it is received by the person you are sending it to. To finish, thank your angels and guides for their assistance, and visualize your energy returning to you.

You can even send a Chi ball to your Self; the process is the same only you visualize yourself receiving instead of another person. When it comes to handing it over to the Archangels, visualize and sense them holding the chi ball you created, feel them pouring the energy over your head like a waterfall of liquid light. Feel the warmth of the energy, flowing through your whole body in waves. You can direct this flow by focusing your awareness on it.

The Angelic messengers, who include our guardian angels, are always with us. Each angel or divine light being has its own 'signature', meaning an identifying color and vibration frequency. Because they are on a much higher frequency than us (while we are experiencing life through our physical body and personality) we will experience them as flashes of different colored lights around us that we can see out of the corner of our eyes.

We can tune into them by honing our 'listening' skills, our Higher Sense Perception of feeling, vision, hearing and knowing. Know that when we work with the Angelic messengers of God, we are automatically protected. The angels have a loving, guiding presence that fills us with warmth and love. Always give thanks and gratitude to the angelic realms whenever you sense their presence in your life, and whenever you have asked for their assistance.

The more we work with the angelic realms, the more we come to notice, and the more we experience them around us. If you feel warmth in certain areas of your body, especially around your head, shoulders, and hands, this is a sure sign they are trying to get your attention. When they touch your face and hands, it feels like soft feathers or little touches. There is nothing to fear from these loving guides, they are not 'loud', they resonate with our heart frequency and by tuning in to our heart we tune in to them. Often, when we are in our heads, we cannot connect with the angels because we switch off the 'receiver'. It is important to be open to the angelic realms if we are to experience and allow them, to interact with us.

Always remember to thank your angels after you have worked with them.

Archangel Michael/Mikhael serves from the Blue Ray of protection and power. He is the Archangel who people generally experience first because he is the 'God of Armies', helping to cut through illusion and helping us to stand in our own power. Archangel Michael's aura color is a royal purple that's so bright, it looks like cobalt blue. He radiates a golden light that makes him appear tanned and blond.

Archangel Michael carries a sword with him. Michael's sword helps us to cut away any negative ties to people and situations that may be holding us back in life or relationships with others.

Archangel Michael can also assist in clearing the negativity from a room or building. Visualize Michael surrounded by the blue light of the First Ray, and feel the blue light extend throughout the room or building, cleansing and transmuting as it goes.

Archangel Michael can be called close to you for any reason when you feel afraid or overwhelmed by situations and feeling vulnerable, or for any reason at all.

Of all the angels, Michael has the loudest and clearest voice. He also has a distinctively blunt speaking style. He gets right to the point, but always with love and a sense of humor.

If Archangel Michael needs to get our attention in a hurry, his voice booms with unmistakable clarity. Yet, he can also be softly spoken when the need arises. Most paintings of Michael depict bright light radiating from his sword. Almost like a solar deity, Archangel Michael possesses an energy that feels and looks like rays of sunshine. It is quite common when Archangel Michael is around, to experience hot flushes.

Often when people need assistance, they encounter a person who miraculously helps who is also named Michael, or variations of the name Michael such as Mikhael, or Michel. This is often seen as validation that the 'savior' has been God sent.

Archangel Jophiel serves from the Yellow Ray of illumination and wisdom. Archangel Jophiel helps us to bring light to situations and brings inspiration and understanding in times of conflict

with others. Jophiel can also help if we are taking exams, or working on a project or task, and to help us stay focused. Archangel Jophiel is also known as the angel of beauty. She helps people learn how to think beautiful thoughts that can help them to feel beautiful in themselves.

People sometimes ask for Jophiel's help to discover more about the beauty of God's holiness and to see them as God sees them. She helps people to recognize how valuable they are, seek creative inspiration, overcome the ugliness of addictions and unhealthy thought patterns, solve problems, and discover more of God's joy in their lives.

In art, Jophiel is often depicted holding a light, which represents her work illuminating peoples' souls with wisdom.

To connect with Archangel Jophiel's energy visualize a bright beam of yellow light surrounding you and filling you from your head to your toes with the yellow ray of wisdom and illumination.

Archangel Chamuel serves from the Pink Ray of love. Archangel Chamuel helps in all areas to do with love. Love of self, love of others and to help us bring the experience of love into our life. He will assist to bring more love to us, and help us to feel more loving towards others, especially in times of conflict within relationships. Call upon Archangel Chamuel to help heal your heart and to assist you to feel love for yourself, to fill your heart, mind and soul with this love. Chamuel will also help you to distribute this love to others in your life and into the world.

Once you feel more loving inside you, you will find that you attract more loving and gentle people to you that you are able to share in this love with.

To connect with Archangel Chamuel's energy, visualize a beautiful and warm ray of pink light surrounding you and infusing you from your head to your toes with the pink-loving light. Feel the pink ray flow through your body and then visualize it being projected from your heart into the hearts of others. Do not discriminate who this love goes to as it is unconditional, and we are connected to all beings.

Archangel Gabriel serves from the White Ray of purity and harmony. Archangel Gabriel assists us to develop a closer relationship with the spiritual side of life to be more of service in the world, to improve communication within relationships to promote harmony within, and to help us to express harmoniously with those around us.

Archangel Gabriel also helps us to improve our talents in all areas of life.

Call upon Archangel Gabriel when you need assistance on the spiritual path and to help bring harmony into your life and relationships.

To connect with Archangel Gabriel's energy, visualize a brilliant pure ray of white light surrounding you from your head to your toes to infuse you with purity and harmony, and to be able to express joy and love to those around you.

Do not be afraid to ask Archangel Gabriel to be with you and accept the purity and harmony with the love that it is being given.

Archangel Raphael serves from the Green Ray of healing and truth. Archangel Raphael's color is emerald green.

We can call upon Archangel Raphael for anything to do with healing. We can ask Archangel Raphael to help heal someone else, but he will not interfere with the other person's free will choice to receive it or not, so it cannot be forced on another unwillingly or unknowingly. It is wise to always ask first, before sending healing energy to others.

Archangel Raphael can also help to heal pets and animals, including wild animals. His gentle energies are welcomed by them.

To connect with Archangel Raphael's energy, visualize his emerald green Ray infusing you from your head to your toes, filling you with the beautiful warm healing light, releasing any pain and suffering you may be experiencing, whether mental or physical.

Archangel Uriel serves from the Gold Ray of peace. Archangel Uriel helps us to find peace within. If we feel conflict with people, we can visualize Uriel's golden light of peace to surround us, then visualize the light radiating outward to bring calm to the situation. Uriel can also be called upon to assist in world situations involving the weather and natural disasters.

If you feel conflict with people around you simply visualize Archangel Uriel's Gold Ray surrounding you from your head to your toes with the beautiful and peaceful ray of golden light, helping you to feel calm and at peace no matter what the situation outside of you.

Archangel Uriel can also help us to send peace out into the world. Visualize the earth surrounded by Uriel's Gold Ray of light, feel and see the gold energy permeate everyone and everything on the surface and underneath the surface of the earth.

Archangel Zadkiel serves from the Violet Ray of freedom. AA Zadkiel assists us to release negativity and fears and helps us to find freedom from negative and fearful situations. Calling on Zadkiel's violet ray brings a higher awareness that is cleansing and illuminating, helping to lift our energy into a more spiritual awareness of being. This violet light may then be extended to others and the world.

When we call upon Archangel Zadkiel and the Violet Ray, we are bringing changes and transformation to prepare for a more spiritual future for mankind.

To connect with Archangel Zadkiel's energy, visualise the violet ray of light surrounding you from your head to your toes, releasing negativity and fears of the lower vibration, and transmuting it helping to lift you into a higher realm of being, removing the effects of all that has held you back from your inner freedom to live purposefully.

Biography - Karen Tants

Karen Tants is a spiritual self-help writer, ghost-writer and author who currently works with authors and compilers to self-publish books and anthologies at Healing Pen Publishing. Karen has helped publish, as well as co-author in, Sundi Sturgeon's Warrior Women with Angel Wings anthologies; Jill Rhiannon's Reading Between the Signs, and Calling All Earth Angels and Healers by Geri Magee, Ph.D.

Karen has a background in healing and working with the angelic realms for the highest good.

Connect with Karen on Facebook:

www.facebook.com/karen.tants

www.facebook.com/intuitiveediting/

www.facebook.com/The-Wisdom-Portal-271720116200807/

www.facebook.com/templeofpeaceangels/

The Transforming Power of "I Am"

By Dr. Sundi Sturgeon

The universe, including yourself and your life, is composed of an all-encompassing Divine Mind, its thoughts and thoughtforms.

On a holistic level, the power of the "I Am" presence has been one of my biggest teachers and wealth activators.

For my chapter in Calling All Earth Angel's and Healer's, I choose to briefly share with you the meaning of the powerful, "I Am" Presence: "I AM." These are the most powerful words you can say. Why? Because "I AM" precedes the subconscious beliefs that you program yourself with, thereby literally telling yourself how to feel in your body, mind and heart.

These words also instruct the greater mind, the universe, to inform an outer reality to match whatever word you choose to insert after the words, "I AM."

What are you saying to yourself? Pay attention not only to the words but also to your thoughts! How often do you find yourself saying, "I AM" angry, or "I AM" sick and tired of...; or some other formation of words that are opposite of how you really want to feel?

What if, you remember the truth of who you are instead, and begin to think and speak from the truth in your heart?

You are the ONLY one who gets to decide on the words that come next after you declare "I AM". Choose wisely. You believe what you tell yourself.

Instead, choose the truth. I AM Love. I AM joy. I AM peace. I AM Powerful. I AM wealth. I AM grateful, I Am spirit, and so forth. That is the truth of who you are after all, and this does not mean that you ignore the other thoughts and emotions you are experiencing; it simply means that you are instructing yourself to remember who you are, what you really desire; whilst declaring to yourself that you are choosing what is true, and instructing the universe to match that instead of all those other things you used to tell yourself.

Now, moving forward, we know that all thoughtforms carry a frequency or a wave-type vibration – tone. Invisible to the eyes as it may be, the energy is alive and very real. These energies can be felt as well as measured. When you hold a pure thought for just over 60 seconds (as explained by Esther Hicks and Abraham for 68 seconds), it is called the 'power of 68', you activate a vibration within you, and the law of attraction begins to respond to that vibration and/or words. When you remember that words carry thoughtforms which are vibrations/frequencies, then you are off and running; whether it is something you want or do not want, the universe will provide.

This is an excellent and powerful way for us to manifest what we desire in a short amount of time by implementing the power of "I AM" into our daily practice.

We are *creating* all the time – only subconsciously. If we direct these thoughtforms of energy by *consciously* focusing on our highest positive intent, we are manifesting for our highest good. We are born co-creating and came forth to be a 'director of energy'.

How do you know if you are holding onto a thoughtform or not? Well friends, by getting sensitive to the way you are feeling because, with practice, you will learn to feel the fluctuations of the vibrations/energy within you.

Your emotional guidance system, in other words, the way you FEEL, is the way you know how you are doing. Play with your thoughts to learn the feelings associated with low vibrational thoughts and words. These low vibrational thoughts and words are counter-productive to your true desires, and they weigh heavily on our body and mind.

As we become more and more aware and conscious of our thoughts, words and feelings, we create from a new space (paradigm) and become mindful of how we interact within all our relationships. Sometimes it may feel as if we are separate from our interactions (as if we are watching; like an actor in a scene from a movie), observing and unsure of our next move/word/action, because we view from the higher perspective of our own truth; and hesitate to co-create especially if we feel we are not in alignment with our inner 'truth detector'.

The law of attraction and Quantum Physics show us the power of intent and observation. One must tune in to infinite possibilities; when people play/ focus/ intend on something, change can be accomplished.

WE can accomplish this in every area of our lives, subsequently activating the 'Wealth of our DNA'.

I would like to share a bit about myself; I AM a teacher and a student of the 'power of intention' and 'higher consciousness' living. Having learned through much trial and error and hardship, I began noticing many years ago a pattern that came along with my thoughts, words and feelings. I was creating many times what was not of truth, or of my real desires. I became conscious of this and began playing in the 'field of possibilities' by using my I AM statements more wisely. Through prayer and awareness, my world and experiences were evolving and shifting. I was learning a deeper understanding, and as I practiced daily, other consciousness teachers began appearing in my life. To coin a phrase, it is truly: "When the student is ready, the teacher appears."

In our holistic and higher consciousness living and healing center, Holistic Light Rejuvenation Center, we enjoy working with our clients on many levels, including using and understanding the power of the "I AM" Presence, power of intention, and by using these proven principles you can heal your life holistically and create who you truly were intended to be, on this earth, right now!

WE integrate these intentions and affirmations whilst our clients enjoy a field of coherent energy that is realigning their original divine blueprint, rejuvenating and energizing their cells. "**Holistic Regenesis**" is truly the future of medicine across the world.

I encourage you to learn about the amazing work we do to assist in raising the consciousness and healing capabilities that you embody, and that is inherent within all humankind to unveil the integral piece of the puzzle that leads to your highest purpose contained within your own being. Visit us at: www.holisticrejuvenate.com

Part of the process we offer our clients is what we call the 'intention board' during their healing experience; be it for mind, body, etheric layers, or emotional wellbeing. This coherent energy field is relaxing, interacts with your innate higher intelligence, synchronizing the hemispheres of your brain.

By using your "I AM" statements and Presence, you are affirming to yourself, and although this may not be true yet-the value is we are preparing ourselves for success.

I would like to give you an example: A very important study and experiment were performed by the brilliant author Dr. Masaru Emoto. In one of his books "Hidden Messages in Water," he shares some incredible experiments that were created using words, and how certain words affected water crystals resulting in either pure, clear sacred geometric formations, or fractured, dark and chaotic formations.

I am referencing Dr. Emoto[2] to show you the value and power of words, and how the vibrations that different words contain have an effect on water crystals that either create fractures, sadness and disease, while holistic words such as love, joy, beauty, peace and wholeness create beautiful formations. By using the word 'hate' either written or spoken, the crystal formation was fractured. Using the words love, joy and peace, the water crystals formed beautiful, whole and complete geometric shapes. Our bodies are comprised of approximately 88% water. Can you imagine then the effect on our bodies from the choice of thoughts and words we use? In this way, we are responding in a fractured or holistic way to our words, thoughts and environment thus creating our experiences. Dr. Masaru Emoto's work is phenomenal. He is highly noted on this subject of the effects of water, of thought forms and the frequency and energy they carry. Positive words express the most-pure high energy and carry the power to create/manifest your dreams. Destructive words create fractures in our lives and bodies; these words *draw* negative experiences to us.

I would now like to share an example from a client experience with learning and understanding the power of her thoughts/ words and the I AM presence in her life. Trauma took her down a path of destruction as it did many times.

We will call her "Angie" in this story. Angie was jealous of others and had much fear. She would use low

---

[2] https://thewellnessenterprise.com/emoto/

energy vibration words and expressions such as 'life is not fair' or 'I am so afraid' or 'I never have enough of anything' which resulted in unhappiness and dissatisfaction; among other dis-eases. As a result, happiness eluded Angie. After a few sessions of Holistic Regenesis, learning the power of, I AM, and using the intention board, her innate intelligence kicked in and she began to shift. Her first biggest shift was during a session she heard in her mind and heart; "Let it Go." She then began affirming daily, easily and began to receive insight from unexpected sources. Angie began using power affirmations such as 'I AM safe', and 'I AM powerful', among others.

In a short time, Angie's life and direction shifted in a very positive way. She became consciously aware of how her thoughts and words had been deeply affecting her life on all levels; including her health and physical well-being. With this new and profound understanding, Angie was 'off and running', effectively creating what she truly desired. Through 're-programming' herself and upgrading old belief systems, Angie soared higher and higher into the direction of her dreams, with major health improvements.

What we can learn from this is that by using disempowering and destructive phrases such as I AM weak, I AM sick, I AM angry, etc... is counter-productive to who we truly are and were meant to be. Trauma and disillusionment in one's life can set us up for a downward spiral and we all know emotional destruction. We then find ourselves creating dis-ease on many levels.

You get the picture; low vibration thoughtforms reinforce victim mentality. However, high vibration thoughts and words create a victorious life.

I encourage you to use powerful (power-filled) statements such as:

I AM perfect, whole and complete.

I AM Love,

I AM abundance in all things for my greatest good.

I AM Joy, thus activating Holistic Wealth DNA; creating a cascade of abundance, effectively creating all you desire, open and ready to receive all the blessings you deserve and were meant to receive.

My sharing with you would not be complete if I did not include some wonderful new research by **www.heartmath.org** on the mysteries of the heart.

Whilst researching these mysteries, Heartmath explains how the heart plays an extraordinary (if not integral) role in our lives far beyond what has been discovered in the past.

The following is what Heartmath have discovered:

- Your heart emits electromagnetic fields that change according to your emotions.
- The human heart's magnetic field can be measured up to several feet away from the body.
- Positive emotions create physiological benefits within your body.
- You can boost your immune system by conjuring positive emotions.

- Negative emotions create nervous system chaos, but positive emotions do the opposite. (remember the effect of thoughts and words on water crystals)
- The heart has a system of neurons that have both short, and long term, memory, and their signals sent to the brain can affect our emotional experience.
- In fetal development, the heart forms and starts beating before the brain is formed.
- A mother's brain waves can synchronize to her baby's heartbeats.
- The heart sends more information to the brain than vice versa.
- Positive emotions help the brain in creativity and innovative problem-solving.
- Positive emotions can increase the brain's ability to make good decisions.

These facts were brought to you by the **Institute of Heartmath Research Center**, where ongoing research is being conducted to help explain the connection and the role of the heart in our emotion-based experiences.

As we begin to practice this new awareness daily, our lives shift in profound ways. I, personally, have been on this journey of reprogramming and upgrading my wealth DNA; re-creating my life from victimhood to victorious.

In closing, I would like to say that as these shifts occur, we have now entered a parallel reality containing some empowering truths:

IN my universe, people are happy. I have a strong belief that my positive thoughts and energy can lift others up. These are some truths that you will begin to experience.

WE are co-creating a more loving, beautiful world full of abundance for all, by shifting our realities; our thoughts and beliefs lead us into (and out from) parallel realities and possibilities.

Quantum physics[3] tells us that there is an infinite number of planets and universes and that we move from one parallel reality to another, every fraction of a second. This aligns with the experience of being in the powerfully creative NOW moment, and the infinite pathways (possibilities and realities) that it contains. Wow! Just consider the possibilities with this knowledge and understanding!

We get stuck in different dimensions or lower vibration energies by repeated negative thinking. This is what a rut is: blocked energy with no escape or relief valve. Therefore, create wisely, using higher vibration thoughtforms and feelings, being mindfully aware that our individual perceptions and beliefs, true or false, create our reality.

We are all playing out different 'movies'; we are all here on this earth to experience, to create, and to have fun. Tap into your 'Wealth DNA' through higher vibration living. To do this use your thoughts, words and feelings/emotions that align with the reality you wish to create.

---

[3] https://en.wikipedia.org/wiki/Quantum_mechanics

We are vibrating frequencies of Light Waves of Energy Playing in a Field of Possibilities. God, source our creator, intended for us all to be victorious!

Remember that you *deserve*, and that you are *allowed*, and that you can *have* ALL your heart's desires. (free will), pay close attention to all that you think, feel, say and do! By remembering how to shift focus, you will experience less and less negativity; including all that is undesirable for humanity on earth like war, calamity, catastrophes and struggles. Help to co-create a loving and peaceful world together, one shift at a time.

I AM powerful profound wealth-in-action in my daily life. I empower others to live their highest purpose. And So, It Is!

Biography - Sundi Sturgeon

Sundi's clients describe her as a 'truly gifted earth angel.' Sundi Sturgeon's loving, nurturing and non-judgmental presence is strongly felt by her many clients as she embodies a unique approach; her gift to empower her clients to reach their highest potential in a loving and safe environment is unsurpassed. She provides her clients with all the tools necessary to re-discover a balanced and peaceful state-of-being.

Sundi's passionate nature was borne from enduring many struggles, trials, and travails including traumatic health challenges, overcoming cancer, fibromyalgia, and a variety of addictions and abuses resulting in two near-death experiences and a personal 'dark night of the soul.' These experiences guided Sundi to birth a new belief system, inspiring the discovery of her unrealized potential; finally reclaiming her self-worth and personal empowerment.

Sundi is a certified Reiki Master, Intuitive Empath/Healer, CHT, NHC, and certified Doreen Virtue Angel Practitioner.

Sundi is a wife, mother, and grandmother who is devoted to caring for all Earth's living beings. A resident of Kihei, Maui, Sundi lives with her husband, Joseph.

As Quantum Energy Healing practitioners, Sundi and Joseph co-founded the Holistic Light Rejuvenation Center, which is a 501c3 educational and charitable organization promoting holistic and cellular rejuvenation services.

Compiler of the *"Warrior Women with Angel Wings"* anthologies, Sundi has also contributed to the following books: *"Women on a Mission," "In the Presence of Angels,"* by Karen Tants, *"How to Get Your Life Back,"* by Brigitte Parvin, and *"Reading Between the Signs;"* a co-authored anthology by Jill Rhiannon.

Sundi is currently working toward her PhD in functional medicine and nutrition; focusing on the silent epidemic of body toxicity and its effects.

Sundi is a globally recognized specialist and intuitive advisor in the field of Integrative Medicine, Rejuvenation, and Quantum Holistic Wellness.

https://www.facebook.com/AuthorSundiSturgeon

www.holisticrejuvenate.com
www.soulpurposemission.com
808-283-7573

Heart Work: Learning to be True to Myself

By Carolyn Osborne

My Earth Angel journey began when I was very small. I just wasn't aware at that time of my true gifts. Seeing spirits and feeling energy didn't translate back then. It was always discounted and 'explained' away. My mother worked in the mental health field and I bet it terrified her. Plus, I was always the different kid in the family; quiet, shy, sensitive and with a different idea of the way things should be. The visions and encounters continued happening but society and those around me did not allow me to acknowledge my gift. I have always had a tender heart, felt others' pain and tried to help them.

As time passed, I began to honor and validate my experiences. As I grew older, my confidence in my abilities grew, along with a change in my societal thinking. I learned that it is important for me to be true to myself and be the earth angel who I am.

My life was consumed in wanting to be an artist. I could nurture my being within my art. You could say it was my 'safe zone'. I had a younger sister and brother who were very different from me. However, all of us were smart and accomplished in different ways. For me, my art was always my shining moment.

My family has always been quite small. I had a wonderful grandma who I adored and when she would give me a hug goodbye, she would always whisper in my ear, "I love you best." Of course, I always thought she said that to my brother and sister too.

In 1990, I had my daughter, Anjelica and oh, did my grandma loves her! At the time, my grandma was in a nursing home and her health was failing rapidly. So, every day I would bring my baby to visit her great grandma. One evening, when Anjelica was five months old, I left her with my mom and she took her to visit grandma. Suddenly, at this event I was at I knew my grandma had just died. Rushing to the nursing home, I found my mom with my sister; they were shocked to see me because no one had yet called me. I told them I knew that grandma had died. Of course, always the "O.K." look when I would mention these things. I was told my grandma was holding my daughter when she died.

There was one instance when I was lying in bed awake and Anjelica was in her crib. This was about a month after grandma had died. I was laying there and I heard my daughter's bedroom door open, which scared me. I got up, pushed the door open since it was no longer closed shut and standing there at the crib was my grandma. She turned to me with that impish, naughty little grin of hers and held her finger to her lips, telling me to be quiet, and she told me, "everything is fine, love you." I turned around and let her continue her visit with Anjelica. My grandma would visit us often. Always letting us know that she was watching over us.

My daughter also possesses the same gift and she has had the opportunity to see grandma, although she does not appreciate this amazing gift she has been blessed with. I am hoping that someday, Anjelica will embrace it.

As mentioned previously, all throughout my life I have seen spirits. To my knowledge, I did not know who they were. And I do remember being terrified. My family would tease me about being afraid of the dark, they just didn't believe the things that I told them. Finally, I stopped telling them and I would lay in bed, my heart beating out of my chest, hoping for morning to hurry up and come. *Now*, when I don't know who is visiting, I am fine with that.

My brother became ill with cancer. It was horrible, he was so young, he battled it for eight years. He was an incredible human, dad, husband, brother, son, friend, and businessman. Sadly, on August 20th, 2008, three days short of his 42nd birthday, he died. That day I will never forget. At 4 am my brother appeared and told me that he was gone. I went into my daughter's room and told her that we need to get up and get dressed so we would be ready when they call us. I told her that David had come and told me he was gone. We were ready when they called at 10 am to tell us David had died. David visits often to this day. My daughter asked Uncle David to stop visiting because it is too upsetting for her. I, on the other hand, relish those visits.

The pain of losing David, my little brother, was so horrible. I wanted to do something that he would have loved. He loved glass, and being an artist who works in glass, I decided to add ashes to glass in his honor. I even had the opportunity to discuss my plan with him while he was still on this earth. He thought it was cool. The first Sacred Embers were created with our sweet dog, Amazon's ashes. She was an incredible "sister" to my daughter. That Rottweiler and Anjelica were quite the duo. She still visits, too.

Sacred Embers was born due to the death of my brother. And in my pain, I found peace with Sacred Embers. With each Sacred Embers that I create for others, I find more peace; I experience the gift of others sharing their loss and pain and intimate memories and thoughts of their beloved person or their pet who has died. Every Sacred ember that I create, I meet with the client in person if they are local or communicate with them however necessary. To hear all about their beloved is such an important part of the process. I truly gain energy from that, which helps to customize their Sacred Embers. Often messages are sent to me or to the client. It is amazing to share those moments as well.

Now, because of all the deaths, I have worked with and my openness to them, I have visits from so many pets and people. I love it. I am honored. I know that my brother is proud of me and the work I do with Sacred Embers.

Biography – Carolyn Osborne

Carolyn Osborne always knew her entire life that she wanted to be an artist. She was born and raised in Tacoma, WA. She attended the Art Institute of Seattle but also attended college for Law Enforcement because she wanted to help people. She was a Corrections Officer for twelve years and in that time brought art to the inmates in her facility. She was always aware of the healing properties of art.

Carolyn says that her greatest creation is her daughter, Anjelica, whom she raised herself. When her daughter was four, Carolyn became self-employed and was initially a partner in a sign company and a few years in decided to go on her own with her own sign business. All the while continuing to create her art and have two art shows per year in her home. Carolyn works in many mediums, including charcoal, watercolor and later fused glass and jewelry. And she keeps adding to her creative repertoire.

When her little brother was losing his battle against cancer at the young age of 42, she knew she needed to find a way to honor him. He loved glass, so Carolyn decided to add ashes to glass. And Sacred Embers was born. The first Sacred Embers items were created in 2009, beginning with her dog, Amazon's ashes. Later came the pieces to honor her brother. In this, Carolyn found that it brought peace, soon realizing she could help others with their grief by creating custom Sacred Embers. No Sacred Embers is created without her taking the time to get to "know" the person or pet who died. She meets with local clients in her home and for those who live afar, she connects via phone and emails. Hearing the memories and thoughts from her clients she considers to be a huge honor and she gains special energy to create Sacred Embers from these interactions. Watching a Sacred Embers client literally change before her eyes, she says, is truly priceless.

Carolyn was also born with the gift of seeing spirits. As the years have gone by, she has learned to honor this gift and often is able to give her Sacred Embers clients messages.

In 2012, Carolyn opened Creative Forces Gifts & Sundries located inside Hotel Murano in downtown Tacoma. This was the realization of a young high school girl's dream to open a shop filled with 100% local artist's creations. Upon opening, she had twelve artists and presently has over sixty.

She is a participating artist in SHEnlightens: A Women's Collaboration Art Project by Amanda L. Gamble. This is a group of women artists creating art representing little-known and known women of history.

Carolyn Osborne
253-227-8871
carolyn@creativeforcesbycarolyn.com
carolyn@sacredembers.com
www.sacredembers.com
www.creativeforcesbycarolyn.com
www.facebook.com/sacredembers

www.facebook.com/creativeforcesllc

430 Berkeley Ave   Fircrest, WA 98466
*by appointment only

My Inner Healer

By Ladonna Nelson

Are you seeking to alleviate suffering associated with pain and illness, whether it be physical, emotional, mental, or spiritual?

Have you suffered a breakup, a job loss, the death of a loved one or a physical injury to your body?

At times like these, finding a balance between recovery and adaptation to your new reality can be challenging to achieve, often leaving you in more despair, especially if you can't find help.

Reiki and Energy Healing strives to create the perfect balance between all elements of the body and soul through a holistic approach.

We liken Reiki to a wave running through our space-time continuum that integrates a patient, disease, healer, reiki, and energy healing working in tandem towards an improved quality of life.

In the past, when interacting with people of all ages who were in pain or suffering of some kind, I would often think, "If only I could help this person feel better." One day, I decided it was time to act, and not to continue wishing any longer. Having grown tired of not doing anything constructive to help others, I decided to do some research; soon discovering there is a lot of information out there if we only choose to look in the right direction, or 'outside of the proverbial box.' I began to attend classes, read books and learn everything I could about holistic healing.

When I first began my research into energy healing, there was very little information on the healing benefits of crystals, reiki, and so much more. In the small town where I lived, many would say, "You do what?" They thought I was full of nonsense; add in the phrase' Angel card reading' and I got even more people thinking I'd lost my mind.

For me, however, I believe in my angels and ask them to guide me when helping others who also believe in angels. Respecting others' beliefs, I omit the cards and all references to angels during their healing for those who don't believe in angels.

People who are open to Oracle and Tarot card reading may call upon me for guidance. If you would like the assistance of the angels in your card or healing sessions, you can choose to have them included, but if not, that is fine as well.

You may not be able to see how the healing process works exactly. Like your cell phone or a radio, you may not know exactly how they work, but we rely on them, and we know they are doing what we need them to do. It doesn't matter how they do their job, just to know that they are working for us. It is the same with Reiki and Energy Healing. We know it's a life force that connects all of us together. Just because we don't know how Reiki or any energy healing is able to work, that shouldn't stop us from using it. By trusting in Reiki & Energy Healing, you can improve your life and the lives of others.

By studying and working with Reiki and Energy Healing, I have noticed the positive changes in my life and others' lives. Through continued remote treatments on others, I have seen how Reiki and Energy Healing has changed their lives for the better. Thankfully, I have been guided to those who have allowed me to help them. I've been able to help many change their lives for the better, physically, mentally, emotionally, and spiritually.

The most rewarding part of what I do is when someone gets in touch with me to let me know they are feeling so much better, or to tell me they are now feeling confident in helping and teaching others to use this special gift that is so easy to learn and use in daily life. All one needs is an open mind and to let things flow.

Success story for a remote healing session (for a human)

A lady reached out to me with severe neck and back pain. She requested distance healing to help with pain control and accelerate healing. After one treatment, the pain that had been there for approximately two months was completely gone. Distance was not a problem in the healing process.

Success story for hands-on treatment (for an animal)

Just like humans, animals also benefit from Reiki and Energy Healing. I noticed the dog was scratching and flipping its head often. When I investigated the ear, it was red and scaly with a bad odor. I performed a hands-on treatment and the dog responded favorably. Later, I returned to do a follow-up treatment. This time, the dog nudged my hand, wanting to feel the same energy that she had previously experienced, relaxed and then fell asleep under my hand. After a week, all symptoms were gone.

Each experience has made me appreciate the opportunity to make a positive difference in someone's life. Delivering treatments and card reading for others and seeing or hearing of the positive changes are so rewarding.

Teaching Reiki and Energy Healing is a passion of mine, for there are so many people who need help. It could be something very simple: by knowing how to help themselves or someone who is ill or suffering, their health can improve quickly, saving them from missing work, school or feeling under the weather. If someone is experiencing something much more critical and life-threatening, doctor care is absolutely recommended. Working in partnership with a doctor, someone who knows Reiki and Energy Healing can assist a person to heal at a faster rate. My passion is to teach as many people as possible how Reiki and Energy Healing can help them personally, as well as help those around them.

Everyone is born with the right to be healthy and happy; that's what Ladonna's healing and reading therapy sessions hope to fulfill. Our treatment goes deep within the mind, body, and spirit to help relaxation, increase vitality, and promote and speed healing.

If you have any questions or concerns about your life, please reach out to me. I would love to assist you in giving you an Oracle or Tarot reading, or just giving clarification to some of your burning questions that can help ease your mind.

Biography-Ladonna Nelson

Ladonna has had the opportunity to work with many people of varying age groups and personal circumstances. Her own family struggles with health issues added to her wanting to make a difference. She enjoys teaching others how to help themselves and those they love and feels the more people we can reach and teach, the stronger our world will become.

With all she has learned and continues to learn, it has been an amazing adventure that she never would have known existed if those she had loved didn't have the health issues they had and for the many who came to her to ease their suffering.

Holistic Healing to Ladonna means there are many ways of healing the body by utilizing what mother nature provides that if we only knew how to, they can benefit us in many ways; e.g., crystals, energy, herbs. However, Ladonna recommends consultation with your doctor if you do have any health issues; holistic healing works well in correlation with a Doctor's help when it comes to learning how to use what mother nature provides to enable us to heal ourselves.

Ladonna is now living her passion as a Holistic Healer. Her path has been born of a deep inner desire and calling to help others to heal and feel better within themselves. To connect with Ladonna or to book a healing or reading, please visit:

www.soulhealingandreading.com

Email: ladonna.shr@gmail.com

Facebook: Ladonna's Soul Healings & readings

A Dream or Reality?

By Samantha Forster

09/08/2017

A young girl, lying in slumber. Disliking the dark, a feeling of fright washed over her with a wave of goose bumps tingling from head to toe.

She finds herself gazing at the wall next to her, in fact, she is almost lost in her stare. The wallpaper is old with leaves printed upon it, reminiscent of a forest picture. Leaves of brown and burnt orange, twigs and sticks. Reminding her of autumn, she becomes lost in her thoughts.

A 5th dimension world is unfolding in front of her eyes. A fresh breeze brushes past her face, her body still.

A leaf moves ever so slightly. Her gaze fixed with excitement and her eyes wide in disbelief. The moon that night was full and bright; the beam of the moonlight shining in through a gap in the Curtain, glistening with sparkles and lighting up the new world that had been born. At this moment, the dread and fear of night had disappeared.

The following morning (not remembering when she fell asleep), the girl woke a little confused and dazed. Disbelief washed over her, although butterflies were dancing in her belly; what had happened that night, did it happen? As she got up, she did not speak of this magical moment, it was hers to keep; something that belonged to her. It made her feel safe and free and a little special.

She could not wait for the night to come; the day was far too long for her. Two days before the encounter, she wished her days would never end. Now, she could barely contain her excitement. Would it happen again? Butterflies were back dancing in her belly, the goose bumps came back, and the chill of the unknown brushed over her as she walked up the stairs.

Standing in her bedroom doorway, her room cold and dark, she switched on the light and looked around. The room had no moonlight; she needed it to be exactly as it was the night before, so she pulled the curtain back a little. Although the moon was bright, she could not see the moonbeam. At this moment, knowing that the light had to be switched off, the fear of the night came back, making her shudder. Taking a deep breath, she ran over to the light switch; she hated the night, she hated not seeing, the darkness was her nemesis. Suddenly, her fear was overshadowed by a thought; she wanted to see the wall-world. Knowing that bravery was a must, she took a deep breath in, the light switch under her finger; if she times it right, she could push the switch at the same time as taking a massive jump across the room and then a small leap into bed. 3-2-1-go. She did it! Now in bed with the bedcover over her head, her heart was pounding, her breathing all over the place.

As someone came upstairs to use the bathroom, she took that as an opportunity to lift the covers from her face. When the covers were free from her head, she was shocked to see that she could see almost everything in her room, mainly shadows or outlines of things, but it was not as dark as she expected it to be.

Settling down in her bed, the moonlight lit up the wall just as it had the night before. She began to stare at the wall in the exact place as the night before. Was it going to happen, was it real?

As her eyes grew heavy, she felt a slight breeze. Now fully alert, her eyes were wide open as the moon shone into the room, sparkling as if glitter was falling from the light beam. She was focused on the wall intent on seeing something. Then, just in that moment of anticipation, the leaf fluttered. The sound of rustling could be heard only faintly but she could hear it. The leaf began to move as though it was being lifted off the wallpaper by someone or something pushing it upward from beneath.

In that magical moment, there appeared a small head and a small arm with tiny fingers. The head was the size of my pinkie fingernail. Tiny little features on the face, her/his hair was long and wispy with little antennas poking out of the top of the head through the hair, glittering silver and white wings shining like cobwebs with dew. At this point, the girl let out an enormous scream. She could not believe what she had just seen, rubbing her eyes from the tears she looked and looked and wished, but the thing had gone. She had begun to cry not through sadness, but the moment was so magical and beautiful she felt a rush of faith and love, knowing that what she had set her eyes upon was incredibly special. She did not mean to scream and scare this little being, but her emotions got the better of her as the being looked directly into her eyes almost to her soul.

She was so sorry for scaring the little being, she placed her head on the wall and expressed her sorrow for her outburst.

Soon she fell asleep, to be woken early by the market being set up across the street. She was completely in awe when she finally had the realization that she had been visited by a fairy!

Her family went to the Sunday market, but all the little girls wanted to do was be in her room to see if she would have a visit from the fairy again. That magical moment changed the way she saw the world. This event would be the start of a wonderful journey.

Although the world and words above seem like a story, it is, in fact, a true tale. Although the visits would happen often, she never talked to them using words. They laughed, and she would watch as they sang and danced in-between the leaves and twigs. The forest fairy was my encounter with another world. A world that I had lost;

unfortunately, things began to happen in my life, and I lost my connection with my inner child.

I have only recently started to let people into my world because I believe. I feel strong enough to let my veil fall! We truly do live in a mystical and magical world. The veil is lifting, and I will see my friends again.

03/11/1978

As I sit here in a reflective mindset, I wonder, where do I start? When did it all start? Where do I begin to reveal all my truths and can they be accepted, can they be trusted? I had a fear of my knowing my gift (as I now know it to be); could it help, or would it hinder another's growth?

I recall the first moment this happened: I have always been able to drift from one consciousness to another, timing has never been an issue with me, but for others; they may need a firm account of things. Timing, dates, where-when-and-how? I will do my best to share my experiences that may match synchronicity that has happened in your life that makes you wonder, "Is there something more to this world that we live in?"

I will begin with my very first 'knowing' experience. I worked in the care industry for many years and had many friends from all walks of life; some hated my presence, some fed off my energy. Well, one normal working day, I happened to say to a friend of mine that I saw her pregnant, sitting on the sofa. Now, at the time, she was single and laughed it off. I then began to say that she would meet someone very soon; someone tall, dark and handsome (cliché I know) but she would have to chase him, and she would love him at first sight. Long story short, two weeks later she did meet him, and two years later she had a healthy baby boy. The strange thing here is that she never saw herself in love, nor in fact, had ever thought about children.

My aunt at the time, at thirty-five, was in a new relationship, my other aunt and I were sitting in the living room not doing anything of interest. I turned to her and said I have just seen my other aunt walk through the door with a massive baby bump. My aunt almost wet herself as she knew for a fact that her sister did not want children; in truth, she was told (many years previously) that she may never be able to have children of her own. Two months later, my aunt found out that she was expecting her first (and only) child.

These past few years, many things that I have predicted or spoken of have come back to my earthly mind as a reminder that I have always had this knowing. I met my partner when I was sixteen; I knew I was to have his children – two boys. I fell in love with his soul the very first time I saw him, I could not breathe for a moment; it was as if I had known him all my life!

As a child, I had feelings, dreams, and senses that I did not understand. I would feel people's pain, anger, dislike, hate; you name it, I would absorb it. This led to unpredictable behavior and I hated school. I had no time for it, or the people I went to school with. My life was shitty but that is a book for another time. All of this led to drinking and smoking, class b drugs at a young age, anxiety, and depression. I was sent to see a phycologist when I was thirteen and prescribed Prozac; my dreams stopped, and my senses dulled. At fifteen, I could not take it anymore and left home because the depression was worse, the anxiety was horrendous, and the anger was consuming my very being! Looking back now, I know I was living a lie and that my awakening had been stopped so many times that my soul/higher self was fighting me all the time, every day having the 'fight or flight' feeling! A mush of feelings and thoughts that I just could not understand or even deal with. When I left home, I no longer took the meds, and wallop - it all hit me once more; the senses grew, the knowledge was vast, the feelings were doubled. The day I met my partner, I knew it was back!

I have so much I could share with you; I have so much I want to say. I have condensed what I have to say, and it almost feels that I am leaving you with questions. I worry that it's not enough information, not enough for you to really understand or imagine this 5D world I was lucky enough to be invited into. My story/my truth is so huge it is beyond even my knowledge and understanding. Each day I learn of something just as magical as my first encounter. I have had the pleasure of having the greatest memories of being invited to visit a mystical, wonderful world, full of courageous noble dragons! But, alas, I must leave that for another time. I hate the thought of leaving this with so many skips in it. I feel strongly that the next passage will be of comfort or at least allow you to know that you are not alone in this and what you are going through is very real, very painful, scary and damn right weird at times.

I have a fear of the dark and I did not know why; my siblings did not, my mother did not nor my father. Where did this start? My mother said that one night I woke up screaming that I had dogs and puppies in my room, I was pale, shaking, and crying uncontrollably. I did not know this until I was nineteen! One box ticked, I guess. Later, mum found out from the neighbor on the corner that the man who used to live in the house before us had a female dog and her pups killed, he buried them in the back garden, and that is what I had seen that night! Mum always knew I had something but being part of a family full of Roman Catholics, it was not something that she talked about, or knew how to deal with, so it became hush-hush. The irrational fear grew from then on and stayed with me for years until at age thirty-four I understood more and let the fear go. The path up to this very point in my life has been hellish on the one hand, beautiful and calm on the other.

I feel, I hear, I sense spirit. Although I used to see spirit full-body standing in a room, I no longer see that way; I see them in my mind's eye whenever they want to come through to me [I do have restrictions, spirit never disturb me when I'm resting or sleeping]. I very much would love to gain this part of my gift back, I do feel that because I was traumatized the first time, the universe is waiting for the right time to introduce this part back. I am fine with this and I understand that things take time to re-develop.

Every lesson we go through; the good, the bad and the damn right ugly and painful, we learn afterward that we have grown and that we have learned a valuable life lesson. I wish I could name them all, but every lesson is tailored for the person going through it. The lesson could be a loss, hurt, love, anger, physical, mental and verbal abuse. I have gone through some of the above, if not more. I was an angry person; a lonely person in a crowded room. I sit here today with love and joy in my heart, I learned to accept everything and expect nothing. I have forgiven my past and thank my past for allowing me to grow into the person I am today. I say allow, but, I have always been this person. I was just afraid and never brave enough to live my truth. I apologize for the lack of information on how I got here and how I live my truth; this is a mind filled with so much more than 'I just woke up and I'm me!!'.

One thing I have learned over many years is that from a very young age we are conditioned; this includes family, teachers, the government or society. We lose our connection with the source and the universe and this is no one's fault; some adults have no idea that we live in a world with such promise and joy. Unfortunately, we are somewhat forced to be led by fear, we then live a life based on a fear we have no control over. I had my voice and my light removed from around the age of seven; this is a curtailed time for any child as we are beginning to scratch the very edge of ourselves, starting to find our feet in this world and beginning to understand that the world is very different. They do say that all children are born with the third eye open and connected with our higher selves. I will say this was true for myself, I lost my ability to see the other worlds at the age of seven. This gift returned at fourteen, I then lost it until I was twenty-one, then at twenty-eight, my awakening began. I fought so hard to ignore it, but the universe kept coming back with such strength that I finally found myself surrendering to the unknown.

It was the hardest decision I have ever had to make. I had to learn to forgive my past, thank my past, purge anything from my life that did not serve me with joy. I stopped drinking, started positive thinking, positive gestures, positive affirmation. I had to heal myself, I had to learn to LOVE me; that was the most difficult task of all. Asking the universe for help was easy, waiting for the signs, well that takes patience and allowing oneself to surrender to something you have no control over; that, my friends, takes courage. It is all possible; I live by expecting nothing, accepting everything. Another great lesson that I have learned is that things must fall apart to allow the new to enter. This includes everything; love, jobs, friendship groups, the town where you live, the home you live in. Your feelings and your very own joy may be affected. Never place your happiness on a person, a place, a home, a job, even the things you surround yourself with. We must learn to find joy in the simple things that are around us daily, we must learn to be grateful for the basics in life. Once we learn this, the rest follows: Trees seem greener, the birds louder, the flowers have a new powerful scent, the food we eat fulfills us, we no longer thrive to be popular or wanted. You find that the rudeness of others simply fades away. Your manifestations happen daily rather yearly. Your purpose in life is to be joy and give joy to others. Remember, happiness can be found in a passing moment, and joyfulness is a choice, a new way to live

I wish you all the very best in finding your truth.

Meditate often, sit in silence, cut away anything that does not fill your life with joy, allow yourself to be free, walk barefoot, listen to nature.

God Bless,

Samantha Forster.

Biography - Samantha Forster

I am 40 years old. I have been through my awakening! It took a few years of heartache and life lessons, illness for me to finally accept me and my gift. For those who do not know about this, I no longer live from ego (hate, anger, self-loathing, jealousy, unhappiness). Trust this, it has taken me until the age of 30-35 to get where I am now. Would I have changed it at that time? 100% no. Would I change it now knowing what it was all for and living the outcome? not in a million years. I have written a small piece in story form; I believe that some may need to be introduced to the possibilities of other realms gently, but also letting people (children, adolescents, adults 19yrs to 60yrs+) know they are not alone. The universe has no age limits or restrictions! I could go on forever about events in my life (past present and future), but that is for another time.

I have two sons who are going through their own awakening, it's hard to watch but I know that when this is over, my goodness it will be amazing for them both. Thankfully, I can help through this period of growth, but can I say the process is hard, terrifying, it's a dark place. My eldest son has just begun to see the light - when I say this, I mean he now understands all those dark nights and days. He now understands that we must fall hard for us to learn how to grow and accept our differences, our abilities and how to use the gifts the universe provides us with. As previously mentioned, I have a few medical issues that I now can say I control, and they no longer control my life. It has taken a few years to get to this level of management, but I'm here and it is all thanks to my way of thinking and my way of living and of course the universal support that is there for us all to tap in too. You may have to be guided to the starting point, but once you know where to begin, we all then wake up to a new understanding and that there is more to our universe! Let me just say, I was doubtful at one time in my life, but then we learn the truth that the possibilities are endless.

Both my sons, aged 10 and 18, are empaths. They struggled so much; being an empath as an adult is hard until you know the role and the things to do and not do. At such a young age, they had to learn the hard way. They tried to fit in because the ego-driven world demanded it from them. Of course, this did not sit well, and they developed anxiety (GAD) as they were not living their truth and began acting from the ego (brain) not from the heart, and not following their souls' purpose. Many children are being diagnosed with ADHD and Autism when in fact could they be empaths, healers, mediums, seers, seekers, indigo, rainbow to name a few.

It makes you think!

The Truth Within Me

By Isabella Rose

How do you know if you are an Earth Angel, Healer, or both? It is not as easy as one may think because the discovery of knowing differs for each of us. We are all spiritual beings, here to experience human things.

My inner knowing of who I Am began at a very young age; I knew I was different but didn't have anyone who understood (or to explain to me why I was different) to encourage me to be who I was. Most of my life I struggled to fit in and be accepted; having to hide my spiritual gifts and talents from family and others, and to suppress my voice by conforming to who and what others thought I should be. I share with you my knowing, forgetting and discovery process of reawakening to the Truth of who I Am.

As a young child, I always had an inner knowing. I knew I had a special connection with God and the Spiritual realm. I knew my senses extended beyond the five physical senses of sight, touch, sound, taste, and smell. I was aware I had the gift of sixth sense (my "clair Senses") and my connection to the Angels, Mother Mary, Jesus, God, and other realms. These abilities, along with my visions, premonitions, and knowingness, set me apart from other children my age and even most adults in my life.

I was raised in the Protestant faith, believing that God is loving. Whenever I felt scared or alone (which was quite frequently, having grown up in a "perfect" dysfunctional, alcoholic family), I found solace and nurturing in my Grammie, nature, and the night sky as well as through visions and my connection with the Divine. When I spoke of these experiences to my parents, however, I was repeatedly told, *"you are just a child; no one will believe you"* or *"you have such a vivid imagination."*

I loved reading books, taking dance classes, coloring, drawing, and other creative arts; oftentimes using them as a way of expressing myself. Every year, I looked forward to helping my mom set up her classroom for the upcoming school year, I especially loved putting up the bulletin boards. I loved helping others in any way I could and would help my Grammie hang out the clothes on the clothesline and take them off afterward when they were dry. I would pick strawberries from the strawberry patch in our back yard and help pick blueberries from the blueberry bushes to bake a blueberry pie with my Grammie. I loved helping her bake from scratch. I also enjoyed helping my Sunday School teachers and giving a helping hand at church events as well as becoming a babysitter for the Children's room. In seventh grade, I became a candy striper at the Cranberry Hospital, a chronic care hospital for those nearing the end of life and began volunteering at a local homeless shelter through my youth group at church.

It was around this time that my once rock-solid faith began to crack and shake. I began dismantling and questioning all I had been led to believe. When the homeless shelter shut down, I had homelessness visions and was worried about those who lived there and asked, "what is going to happen to them? Where are they going to go? Who is going to help them? Doesn't anyone care?" I wasn't satisfied with any of the answers I received from the adults I asked but accepted them anyway.

I began to question if everything I had learned in Sunday school was true, shifting my perspective to believe that God wasn't really loving at all but rather cruel and judging. In the youth group, we were asked to draw a picture of how we saw our family in the future. I drew three children, one of whom was handicapped. My teacher reacted with shock, questioning how I could possibly draw one of my children as handicapped. Her disapproval contradicted my firm belief that we are all perfect in the eyes of God.

I began to discern even more who I could share my spiritual gifts with and who I couldn't, sharing them with fewer and fewer, hiding them more and more until I eventually shut them out entirely. Shortly thereafter, I stopped spreading the word of Love. A year later, at the age of fourteen, I was raped by an upperclassman. My father had me talk to his priest, who placed all fault and blame on me. I turned to write poetry and journaling to enable me to express myself without judgment or negative consequences from my father. With each traumatic experience, I became closer to the feminine/motherly archetype of deity and more disconnected from the male archetype of deity. I could no longer relate to God as I had known him and began exploring my Pagan roots. I eventually hid those beliefs too because I got tired of defending them after being ridiculed or called a Satan worshipper.

Although I kept my beliefs hidden, I continued to expand my knowledge and exploration of spirituality and shortly after high school my passion for living an all-natural lifestyle began. I read books on nutrition by Dr. Elson Haas, began seeing a nutritionist and attending weekly yoga classes. I became interested in aromatherapy and began to study it on my own through reading books. Shortly thereafter, I was introduced to Reiki.

I found Reiki very relaxing and helpful on some levels and continued my sessions after my eight-year relationship failed due to my infertility issues and my partner's infidelity; he had gotten another woman pregnant. Just like my premonitions and visions of what was to become of my friend' s marriage when I was a teenager, I predicted what was to come for my former partner when he came to tell me news and ask for my advice. Several years later, those predictions came true also. I was slowly beginning to follow in my parent's footsteps the cycle laid out before me by my parents and ancestors.

I veered off course a little more in my next relationship, following a little more in my parents' footsteps but no matter how many times I veered off course I always found my way back to my faith and my connection to my deity.

In my mid-thirties, I began reconnecting to my soul, the Angelic Realm, and the magic. I wanted to become more involved in the alternative health field and started to consider a career in it although I still had many doubts. I became Reiki I certified and began attending occasional meditation classes. As I learned more about myself, the Angelic realm and my spirituality, I decided I wanted to go back to school. I became a certified Angel Messenger and obtained my aromatherapy certification.

I was completely losing my sense of self in the relationship I was in and knew something had to change. I was living that childhood nightmare and trauma all over again but as an adult with my adult partner. I was in a relationship that mirrored almost exactly the one I saw my parents living when I was growing up. I couldn't take it anymore and began praying, asking my angels, my late aunt and the Universe to give me the courage and strength I needed to learn to love myself and take my power back from those whom I had allowed to control or hurt me. A few weeks later, I set that as my full-moon intention; and so, began my healing journey of body, mind, and spirit to break the cycle of trauma and abuse that ran throughout my ancestral lines for generations.

Over the next twenty-two months, I would change the way I viewed myself and the world around me, taking the biggest risk I have ever made: to allow love into my heart. My "Clair Senses" broke wide open again and I began remembering the Truth of who I Am. It was a very confusing time and very few people understand what I was going through. I was fortunate to have a select few (whom I could completely trust to share my experience with) that I had become close to in my Sisterhood and Lightworkers group.

With Warrior Goddess Training and the Inner Priestess program, I slowly learned to love, accept, and approve of ALL of me – both the light and dark aspects of myself and my past. As I did, I shed the layers of masks I wore, and the fortress of protection I had spent a lifetime building around my heart began to crumble away. I had worn these as shields to prevent myself from feeling the continual hurt, judgment, repeated abandonment, disappointment, and betrayal by loved ones from happening again and again.

With the love, support, encouragement, wisdom, and guidance of my sisterhoods and Matt, the man who would break open my heart to allow love in, I replaced the outdated false belief systems – that I am not lovable, good enough, worthy, or deserving of good things – with the knowledge that I AM.

I saw that I had the same beauty inside and outside of myself that I saw in others and in nature. I was no longer afraid to share my rawness, vulnerabilities, and Truth (my divine and authentic Truth rather than the truth of the false belief systems I once perceived to be true). As I began to trust more in myself, intuition, and divine guidance, I gained confidence and began to feel more comfortable sharing my spiritual gifts and talents, which I had kept locked inside since early childhood. With the healing power of love, I began to make my childhood dreams a reality.

One day, I noticed a Facebook ad asking for contributing authors. Instantly, my heart and soul lit up crying out with excitement and hope, but my ego-mind quickly took over with the false belief systems programmed into my mind since early childhood: *"you can't do this. You're not good enough. Who do you think you are? No one is going want to read your words."* Somehow, I summoned up enough courage to follow my heart, intuition and Divine guidance and reached out to Jodi about my interest in contributing to **365 Moments of Grace**. It was a dare of sorts to myself because deep down, I truly didn't believe they would respond never mind be interested in publishing my writing, but they did! So began the beginning of making not only my own childhood dream of becoming a published author come true but also that of many others.

Tapping into my creativity enabled me to heal and break the cycle as I continued my studies of Angels and Oracle readings with Doreen Virtue. I expanded my studies even further with Melanie Beckler and received my Angel Energy Healer certification.

On December 27th, 2016 I experienced a miracle of Divine intervention and a powerful valiant act of love. I survived what should have been a fatal car accident by the Grace of God and my fiancé risking his own life to help save mine. Despite all the other injuries I sustained, alone, my aorta collapsing in several places should have killed me. Shortly after impact, as I sat in my seat, I started to panic because I couldn't breathe; one of my lungs had also collapsed. *"Remember your angels"* popped into my head, followed by the gentle yet powerful omnipresence of Archangel Michael, *"don't panic. You are safe and protected. Everything is going to be ok."* Almost immediately, Matt was back on the other side of the car, trying to get me out. As I reached out my arm to him, I went unconscious and the next thing I remember I was waking up in the ambulance with an EMT cutting my pant leg off. Confused and not knowing what was going on, I began to panic, screaming for Matt. Once I heard Matt's voice behind me reassuring me that everything was ok and that he was right there and not going to leave me, I slipped back into unconsciousness. I was saved for a higher purpose, a higher plan. I shouldn't be alive today to tell this story.

With the encouragement of my late fiancé Matt (he transitioned to the Spirit realm two months after the car accident) and my occupational therapist, I completed the admissions process and enrolled in the Doctorate/Ph.D. program at Quantum University. With further encouragement from my occupational therapist, I took the knowledge and education I already had in alternative healing modalities and applied it to myself. I used deep breathing, sound frequency, visualization, gratitude towards my body, aromatherapy, Angel Energy Healing, and Reiki to name a few. It was so incredible and amazing when attending follow up visits with my orthopedic surgeon to see validation of scientific evidence and to hear my doctor say, *"keep doing what you are doing, it's working!"*.

I had to (at times) get creative and think outside the box, one day asking my angels for help to figure out how I was going to do certain things having use of only one arm, my non-dominant arm at that.

As I continued to heal and experience the traditional western medicine model, I was more and more rudely awakened to how much it is failing us. I couldn't get answers from testing and traditional doctors and kept getting passed from specialist to the next to the next; none of them finding answers and none of them working together as a team to find answers. Then, add the hassle of insurances, not being able to get a primary care physician, and although asking the hospitals and my vascular surgeon for help in obtaining one; not getting the help I needed. I was getting more and more frustrated and fed up with the system and my medical rights and needs not being met, I again gave up on allopathic medicine and began applying the knowledge and the things I was learning on myself. I always called on my Angels and Matt to help me, heal me and keep me safe and protected. I had a solid faith, trust and knowing they would.

I am fully awakened to the Truth Within Me; I Am a multi-dimensional Spiritual Divine being in human form to carry out my soul's mission and a higher Divine plan that was laid out before the night of what should have been a fatal car accident for me, before my incarnation into this life. I Am an Earth Angel, Healer, Lightworker and Creative among many other things.

Biography - Isabella Rose

Isabella Rose is passionate about the healing arts. She improves peoples' lives through her creativity, writing and healing work by touching upon the innermost emotions, desires and dreams held deep in their hearts, encouraging and inspiring their own creativity and movement towards healing and achieving their fullest potential. She builds community by bringing like-minded people together in her interactive, hands-on workshops, making everyone feel safe, comfortable and included.

Isabella has a diverse and extensive background in various alternative-healing modalities (including Angel Energy Healing, Reiki, Aromatherapy and Braintap Technology). As a holistic health practitioner, she specializes in empowerment and recovery, combining different healing and creative-art modalities with her clients and in her workshops for a unique experience tailored to the individual needs of those she works with.

Isabella is an inspirational writer and contributing author to the bestselling 365 Book Series, contributing to 365 Moments of Grace, 365 Life Shifts: Pivotal Moments That Changed Everything, Goodness Abounds: 365 True Stories of Loving Kindness, and 365 Soulful Messages: The Right Guidance at the Right Time. She is featured in the bestselling book, Soul-Hearted Living: A Year of Sacred Reflections; Affirmations for Women by Dr. Debra Reble. She is the author of the upcoming books,

Behind the Masked Smile: A Survivors Quest for Love and Coming Home: A Journey into Love.

Isabella has also appeared on the Global Transformation Summit as an expert speaker on Angels and Angel Energy Healing.

Isabella lives in New England in a small town near Plymouth, Massachusetts, where she finds much inspiration for her writing and creative arts. She enjoys spending time in nature and with loved ones. Isabella is an advocate for those who feel they have no voice, loves helping others, and volunteers for non-profit organizations close to her heart. Isabella can be found online:

www.bellarosehealinghands.com

Margarita's Story

By Margarita Amrita

My story begins seventeen years ago, after I suffered from postpartum depression following the birth of my son.

Postpartum depression was a silent killer that was not recognized at that time, which caused my whole word to spin around in the most negative way. I felt miserable because I was left in the desert of my suffering, totally unsupported by my family and friends. In fact, I was abandoned and labeled as a negative person, a bad mother and a terrible wife. I was stuck at the dead end, hurt and in the darkest hours of my life, but my responsibility and love for my baby kept me going. No matter what the attitude, I knew I needed to survive for his sake.

At that time, I was prescribed heavy antidepressants and anti-anxiety pills but they left me feeling totally disoriented, tired and withdrawn from life. I started to feel I was turning into a vegetable and that was worse for me than my struggle with depression.

During that time, my sister sent me a book by Tara Ward, "Meditation and Dreamwork." That book was a true treasure. I had never been exposed to Alternative practices, but this book was so easy to grasp and understand that I practiced day and night, feeling better each day. After some time of practice, I experienced spontaneous Kundalini rising. It was incredibly intense! I felt waves of energy going from the top of my head and down to my legs locking the circle of energy into a continuous flow that made me shake and sweat. It was such an unexpected and mind-blowing experience that it took me a while to calm this energy down to stop the cycle, as it had started to get out of my control.

This experience changed my life forever! It's helped me to realize that there is a Universal Life Force beyond our comprehension when we are in the so-called "normal" state of mind: it only gets experienced during intensive breathing, or energy channeling practices.

As a result of this unexpected experience, I've been immediately relieved from depression and anxiety. It was amazing! I could not believe it!! It was so easy to heal overnight after long and painful sinking into the muddy waters of depression. I was so excited about it that I shared my experience with someone important to me at the time; teaching me the hard way that it's better to be alone than to be in bad company. I was getting back to normal and pulling myself together finally!

Since I had my spontaneous Kundalini rising experience, I have been unable to repeat it! I have tried so many times but with no results. However, following my awakening by this mysterious energy, I have wanted to learn more and find a way to expend beyond our limited human comprehension of the world and our conventional understanding of life-purpose.

Since then, I have studied with Zivorad Slavinsky, the author of "Spiritual Technology"; read Vadim Zeland's "Reality Transurfing"; signed up and been accepted to "G. Gurdjieff foundation" of NYC to study books of this remarkable man and his disciples. I have studied in the "School of Images", led by Catherine Sheinberg; the author of "Kabbalah and the Power of Dreaming."

I have been a yoga practitioner for more than ten years and have studied the yogic texts, Bhagavat Gita and "Tripura Rahasia." Thus, I stepped on the road of Enlightenment, left my husband, and fell in love with a man in my yogi community.

However, as time passed, my euphoria melted away when serious problems requested my attention: at the age of 44, my rent had gone up and my boyfriend was diagnosed with cancer, changing the path of my life. My boyfriend moved to California for cancer treatment, so we broke up and I purchased a house near beautiful Raritan Bay. All my practices suddenly seemed like dreams that happened and passed me by, and I again became depressed and miserable.

But being in this depressed state opened my eyes to the realization that I am too much focused on myself and my feelings. I knew women in my community who had lost their houses during hurricane Sandy; some lost their families, kids, and here I was desperate and empty, but I had my son with me, my house, and my community. So, I started to focus on community work. The community work shifted my focus onto other people's needs and that healed my wounds as I felt so much love and gratitude towards women who truly were in desperate need of help.

The serving the community gave me a greater sense of purpose. Thus, I now invite spiritual teachers to our monthly circles, and I arrange events and retreats to help people regain their energy. I met my second husband through one of my workshops; he was a Qi Gong master and I felt so much love and energy coming from him.

Soon after, I learned about Neurographica – the art of positive change. It truly did change my life; forever! Since I completed the instructor's course, I have taught over three hundred people; some of them going on to become instructors themselves. Neurographica allowed me to bring even more value to my community. Soon my Level 1 course will be available on Teachable.com Level 2 is coming up in November - my students are absolutely IN LOVE with Neurographica! I am looking for sponsors, producers, people who are willing to help to spread the knowledge of Neurographica and earn money by pairing with me! I am so open to collaboration!

My first education was as a teacher, but when I came to the US, I had switched to the fashion industry taking classes in FIT (Fashion Institute of Technology) and worked in the Fashion industry for five years before switching to the Project Management career. I have also been interested in philosophy and psychology, taking courses on it (like Process Oriented Psychology by Arnold Mindell). So, I had the idea to combine all my knowledge together: art + teaching + psychology together. Neurographica was able to do all of it for me. It had added Neuroscience on top of it! Now I have arrived at the point where I am allocating full-time for building my school, my courses, my retreats, my offline classes that I am launching with Tibet House of NY led by Robert Thurman (father of Uma Thurman), in November of this year.

My calling is to teach the super innovative method for rapid transformation of humanity - as I find Neurographica to be the most potent method for long term lasting changes, profound changes!

My husband and I have started building the retreat center in Upstate NY – we are currently working on completing the spiritual camp.

Right now, I am expanding my Neurographica coaching practice to teach people around the globe online!

I am happily married to my husband, Yuriy (who shares the following story), my son is finishing college and dating a beautiful girl – Life is Good!

Biography – Margarita Amrita

Margarita was born in the USSR - a country that no longer exists - in the small republic of Uzbekistan, which is now an independent country.

Margarita's parents, then children, were in the summer camps when WW2 started. They had migrated there from Ukraine and Belarus, as Uzbekistan was not impacted by war and it was a safety net for children from all over the country to stay and wait for their parents to reconnect at some point. Her parents were lucky as Margarita's grandparents survived the war and reconnected with their children.

When her parents got married, they both had graduated from college and were working. Margarita's mother built her career by getting her Ph.D. in Biology, and her father built his career in Civil Engineering. So, you would think they were well to do? Not really. In the Soviet Union era, everyone was living on the edge of poverty, no matter what they did!

Four of Margarita's family (her sister, herself and their parents) lived in a tiny one-bedroom house with no bathroom inside the house. Food was always scarce, with their father often stuck in long lines, waiting to get the food basics.

Being raised in this environment was dis-empowering for Margarita! She saw that her parents worked hard just to cover basics and that discouraged her tremendously from taking any steps toward building a career. Yet, she graduated from college, with her professor asking her to stay and teach.

Margarita then got married, with both immigrating to the US to begin a new life. During the next five years, Margarita found work as a waitress in the local pizzeria in Brooklyn, she also sold leather coats while taking an evening class in NYC. Next, she took a career in the fashion business and then switched to Information Technology.

Margarita finally had a son, born after many years of trying and failing to get pregnant. But then, her marriage had fallen apart, she had postpartum depression that went under-diagnosed. All this led to divorce, depression, and struggle.

Margarita survived for her son! With great hopes and big dreams, she could not check out so easy!

The spiritual practice helped her to get through the hardship, find true love and get on the path of Entrepreneurship. Two years ago, she began teaching. Being a teacher by nature and education helped her to come back to herself. Today, Margarita coaches' women who are going through their mid-life passage to find their unique path and stay on it!

She is proud to make a difference in the world!

Margarita A. Schwartzman

Cell Phone: 1-917-572-4343

Email: amarnaneuroart@gmail.com

Website: https://amarnaneuroart.com/

Facebook:

https://www.facebook.com/AmarnaNeuroart/

https://www.facebook.com/amarnasanctuary/

Instagram: @amarna_neuroart

YouTube:

https://www.youtube.com/c/AmarnaNeuroart

How I met my Margarita:
and the incredible healing story that led to a successful and fulfilling marriage

By Yuriy Khomyakov

I met Margarita at a Family Constellation workshop led by my friend at Margarita's house. My friend had invited me because I was seeking a relationship and there were supposed to be several women that might be a good fit for me according to my friend. Also, I had never experienced the Family Constellation work, so I was excited to stop by and participate.

When I arrived, Margarita seemed very sad and mildly depressed. I was not drawn to her at all, as she, herself, looked withdrawn and unapproachable.

Being a professional photographer, I took pictures of everyone and that gave me a chance to collect everyone's information to send them those pictures and possibly set up the dates.

Then one day, just before new years of 2015, my former girlfriend called and invited me to her New Year Party. She mentioned that she misses me and would like to see me – so, I've decided to go and see how things are going with her.

When I've arrived, another man was there who happened to be her current boyfriend. Nobody else seemed to be coming! That was the most ridiculous thing a woman could do. I stayed because at that time I had just sold my car and traveled from Staten Island to Poconos using several public transportations.

When I came back home, I felt very tired, disappointed and somewhat upset. I was no longer in love with this woman, yet, what she did was as ridiculous and stupid as it can be, and it had left a pretty bad taste in my stomach. So, I practiced Qi Gong intensively for the next couple of days to cleanse myself from the negative energy, thoughts, and influences I had experienced at the party.

Around January 5th Margarita called me and asked me to come over to help her with some handyman house herds. She told me that she had asked our mutual friend if anyone can help her to hang curtains in the rooms and our friend had recommended me. So, Margarita and I agreed that I will come over and help her.

While I was hanging the curtains, I was feeling heaviness and emotional disturbance coming from

Margarita. When I've asked what had happened to her, she started crying and told me that she had broken up with her boyfriend because he was diagnosed with cancer, and he had left for California, cutting a relationship with her. Turned out she visited him there but his whole behavior pushed her away and she had returned to NY all torn apart, devastated and utterly unhappy.

I felt a great impulse to help her as much as I could, so I had suggested if she would accept my help, I would come every day and give her Qi Gong healing. She was shocked when I've suggested it, because, according to her, she was working with several healers and shamans with no success.

I've promised her that I would rid her of suffering in a couple of days. She agreed.

So, the next day, we had practiced together and she immediately felt 50% better according to her words after we have completed the practice on the first day. She smiled, giving me a hug and a kiss on the cheek. I was happy she was smiling for the first time since I've known her.

So, I've started coming every day for the next consecutive seven days and she was getting better each day. Yet, we were just good friends! She recommended me to her friend and very shortly my schedule was booked full-time with female clients in need of healing.

However, for some reason I was drawn back to Margarita; although I was not attracted to her as man, she was so smart, witty and caring that I saw her as my true friend and someone I can trust and have fun with.

The time passed by. We've seen each other often and slowly we started developing feelings for each other until one day, she asked me to stay overnight. So, I've stayed!

Since that time, we started seeing each other almost every day. I would work and come back to stay with her. We've traveled places together, made new friends together, creating a community for women who needed help and both have been contributing to the community by providing circles, healing, Qi Gong practice and much more.

We've married the same year of 2015 and our relationship has deepened even further beyond my expectations and my imagination.

We have been together inseparable every day since our marriage. It was amazing that we have never had enough of each other and always things to talk about and share.

Yuriy's Calling

My journey in life has been rocky! Having grown up in a small town in the Ukraine, I could not even imagine that at some point in my life I would live in the United States, where I would meet the woman of my dreams, start a new family, new venture and finally fulfill my calling which I had been denying for years.

Many years ago, I became gravely sick. My brother had convinced me that I needed to start learning and practicing Qi Gong to help me to recover. I was desperate at that point and decided that I have nothing to lose but to take up his offer.

By that time, at the age of forty-two, I was too young to die! I have practiced daily for almost three years, and over the first couple of months of practice, almost fully recovered from my sickness.

Through my practice, I have opened to my higher calling... I had experienced extraordinary out of body events, communicating with higher beings and getting enchanted with energies that would enter my body, healing it and repairing all damaged cells – incredible joyful times!

That is when I had a message from higher beings that I will live a long life, but I must serve. I must teach people, Qi Gong. I must heal them with my energy.

To this end, I started my Qi Gong school teaching in Ukraine first, then I moved to the US, where I have helped hundreds of people who were in a state of despair, enabling them to heal and create new beginnings.

I always wanted to open a retreat center but I could not imagine how! Only when I met Margarita (my love, my life, my earth angel), I've learned that she had this life goal to build and open a retreat center where she could invite her community, teach and invite other teachers.

I was delighted to learn about her aspirations –as they have matched mine! So, when we got married, we discussed our plan to open the retreat center in five years. But, after two years of marriage, we realized that we can't wait and need to move ahead looking for the perfect land!

And, finally, after a long and exhausting search, we have acquired 16,5 acres of land in Cooperstown, NY.

I am now building our life-long dream, ready to invite our first attendees next year. Margarita is working on spreading the word, preparing for fundraising and bringing together a community.

Finally, both of us feel that we are now fulfilling our life mission to enrich the lives of others to grow and heal in mutual harmony.

We will open the doors to the first attendees next April, while still developing other facilities!

Biography - Yuriy – Qi gong Master

What is Qi gong:

Qi gong or Chi Gong (pronounced chee-gong) is an ancient Chinese exercise and healing technique that involves meditation, controlled breathing and movement exercises. These involve simple, slow movements done repeatedly and some static practices as a Big Tree that require being in the static position that is required to be held for 30 + minutes

What is Zhong Yuan Qi gong (ZYQ?) Qi gong is an ancient Chinese art of self-regulation, improvement of one's health and communication with different forms of life. Zhong Yuan Qi gong (ZYQ) represents the highest levels of Qi gong. It has a seven-thousand-year-old lineage and is comprised of the wisdom and knowledge of Qi gong masters from many generations.

The methods of ZYQ allow a human to improve one's health, reach longevity and increase the quality of life. This is the first book on ZYQ from the series "Enter Your Inner World." Reading it and practicing the exercises can help you realize that all forms of life in the universe constitute a whole and that the universe is a living organism of which we are apart. ZYQ is a branch of science through which you can learn how to develop your body, energy, and spirit. This knowledge thus leads to the development of individuals and the evolution of humanity.

The purpose of Qi gong is to understand what Life is by opening our eyes wider to see our world in a different light. Through this system of knowledge and healing, we can open our hearts to understand the many hidden aspects of the Earth and the Universe. Practicing Qi gong can help us realize that all living creatures in the universe constitute a whole and that the Universe is a living organism of which we are a part of. Similarly, our planet Earth is alive, just like us. Qi gong helps us understand the relationship between the whole and its individual parts while enabling us to establish a connection between them.

Yuriy's teacher is Grandmaster Professor Xu Mingtan.

Walking with Angels

By Camille Amos

I have always had a certain sensitivity to what was happening around me. When I was a child, I had what my parents called "an imaginary friend". Well, I know my friend was not imaginary, he was real. He taught me things, and he told me what I would need to know in life. I could see him and hear him. The problem was that my parents couldn't see him. They didn't understand why he would be there. When I was about four, they told me that I would have to send him away so I had a long talk with him and we said goodbye. I was sobbing, I felt like I was losing my best friend forever.

He told me that even though I wouldn't be able to see him anymore, he would always be with me, watching over me, guiding me and protecting me. And he reassured me that every once in awhile, I would hear him whisper in my ear.

Later in life, as is usually the case, life got in the way and the occasions that I heard him whisper to me were fewer and fewer. However, I was still very sensitive about energies and knew things that were going to happen. I never had control in my dream state, to know the knowledge, I knew after one of my detailed dreams that permeated the depths of my soul. Usually, it was information about myself and things in my personal life, especially if I was having a crisis.

One time, however, I saw and heard a crime in progress in my psychic state. It seemed so real that I went outside to see if I could help. There was a young woman in trouble. When I got outside, I couldn't see or hear anything unusual. It was quiet and calm. Then in the morning, on the local news, I heard about the crime and saw the face of the young woman that I had seen in my vision. For months, I tried to follow the clues to be able to help find her. I was getting crazy from the restlessness I felt as well as the lack of sleep. This wasn't the first time this had happened to me. There had been several of these incidents before and I found them to be very unsettling. I asked God to remove this burden from me. I told him that if I couldn't be of assistance to the people involved, I would really rather not have these experiences. The next ten years of my life were pretty quiet.

Then, gradually, I began to "tune in" more, to attempt to listen to my own inner voice. I started writing down my dreams in a dream journal (something I hadn't done in years), and I tried meditation. I had never felt like I was very good at meditation because my mind just wouldn't get quiet.

Then a few weeks ago, something extraordinary happened to me. I had gone to a friend's house because we were going to attend a therapy session later that day. It is something we have been participating in for the last seven or eight months, known as Family Constellation Therapy – mainly for the purposes of personal growth and spiritual development. Whenever we go, I always invite my spirit guides, my guardian angels, and my ancestors to come with me and join in the healing sessions. And of course, I always ask God's blessing on all that will take place. This process has been rewarding and energizing.

This particular day, however, my friend was in a lot of pain. She wasn't sure that she would be able to go. She decided she needed to rest, so she went to her office and laid down on the sofa. I stayed in the living room and said a little prayer for her. I was very sure she was going to be ready to go soon. Then, I put my legs up, leaned back on the sofa, got comfortable and took a few deep breaths. I was just planning on resting while she rested. As soon as I closed my eyes, I began to see images. I moved in to get a closer look.

One of the images was a Native American Chief with a headdress of feathers and traditional deerskin clothes, just like the Native Americans I had seen at the Pendleton Round-Up when I was four. We lived in

Pendleton, Oregon at the time. The night before the Round-Up, my dad took us to see the Teepee Village where the Native Americans were camped. The men had been wearing white, brown or black leather shirts and pants with bead-work and lots of fringes. Most of the women wore white leather dresses with elaborate bead-work and turquoise jewelry – necklaces and bracelets. They were smiling as they danced around the bonfires. In fact, whole families were dancing together around the fires. I saw their teepees. They looked so much bigger close-up. Their chanting to the rhythm of the drums reached right into my heart. They were chanting Hey ya, hey ya, hey ya, hey ya, HEY. Hey ya, hey ya, hey ya, hey ya HEY... and dancing. It was hypnotic.

Since we lived so close to Teepee Village, when I got into bed I could hear the drums and the chanting for what seemed like hours. I imagined them dancing around their fires all night long while the flames shot up to the beating of the drums. Finally, I happily drifted off to sleep with the drums and the dancing and the flames. Hey ya, hey ya, hey ya, hey ya. HEY. Hey ya, hey ya, hey ya, hey ya HEY. Hey ya, hey ya, hey ya, hey ya, HEY. Hey ya, hey ya, hey ya, hey ya HEY....

That was then. Now, as I move in to get a closer look at the chief, to my surprise, I see my face, on him. He is older than me. He looks strong, confident. He looks-wise. He is holding a dog on his lap. It's a beautiful white dog with long hair. I can feel his love for this dog. He is very proud of it and takes very good care of it. He has kept it separate from the other dogs of the tribe so that it wouldn't breed with them. He wanted its fur to be used for weaving the ceremonial blankets of the tribe. He knew that the way to measure a person's wealth is not by how much they have, but by how much they have to give away.

I found out later in life that the Salish Indians who lived in and around Puget Sound had Woolly Dogs that they sheared twice a year to use their fur for weaving blankets. [These dogs have been extinct for more than a hundred years. They looked exactly like the one the Chief had on his lap].

He actually looked right at me and smiled. He knew why I was there.

Now I knew why, too.

When I was seven, I had a near-death experience. I didn't understand it that way at the time, I was a kid. I had encephalitis and was hospitalized for a couple of months. My time in the hospital is vague, but I remember God showing me around heaven. I remember Him telling me that I would live and that He had a special mission for me on earth. I asked him what it was. He said I would know when it was time.

Until now, I hadn't been sure what my mission was. I tried to tell my mother and father about my experience, but I had a hard time communicating what had happened to me. I had aphasia which meant that the words I would try to say came out as other words. I knew exactly what I wanted to say but could not make myself understood. It was like I would think "banana" but what would come out of my mouth would be "train". My second-grade teacher came to my house every day, a true earth angel, to help me to read and talk about what I was reading and just to spend time with me. She was such a loving person. I will never forget her for that. She was a very special part of my recovery.

And now, as the Chief faded out of focus, I saw images of people flash in front of me, one after the other from different periods in history. Each one of them had my face! Male-female; old – young; white – black, everything in between, all races, religions, everything you could imagine; very rich – very poor. As I looked at them, I could feel everything they were feeling. Everything. What fascinated me with all of these people was that the ones who were the happiest were the ones who had the fewest material goods. The ones who had the most were scheming to find ways to have more. There was so much fighting, with many attacks on innocent victims. Some of the fightings were on one, some of it was in small groups and I didn't understand all of the violence.

Then another image pulled into focus. It is me as a male, a private in a Union Soldier uniform during the Civil War. I had a gun – a rifle. And I had a sword in my belt. There was a rectangle of black tape over my mouth – as if I was not supposed to say anything – just follow orders.

We all know about the horrors of the civil war were at times, brothers were actually fighting brothers. We know that this war divided the nation it was trying to unite in ways that are still visible today while attempting to make free men of slaves. So, I won't go into all the contradictions or the details of what I saw. Suffice to say that all of the men in both Union and Confederate uniforms had *my* face. When it was over, I saw myself standing over my own body. I could feel the coldness of death settling in. But, I was alive even though I was dead. I was me and yet I was *every* man. And now, I was finally free to tell what I had witnessed.

This scene slips out and I see scenes very much like this all over the world in different time periods:

WWI, WWII, The Revolutionary War, The Crusades... centuries of wars without end.

The reasons for war, however, always get blurred. In the beginning, it all seems very clear, but when the casualties begin to mount, all we feel is the anguish at the loss of our loved ones, our way of life or any plans we may have had for the future of ourselves or our families. It is time to put an end to proclaiming that it is our "sacred honor" in order to get good men and women to go into the nightmarish battle of needless violence.

Suddenly, I have pulled away from these visions of war and the endless crimes against humanity. I am lifted from the depths of this darkness. I feel a sense of peace flooding over me. I surrendered to the waves of energy flowing through me, renewing me. Love was radiating from me in all directions.

I see people meditating.

I hear chanting, prayers and singing that sound true to my soul...

Om

Omni Podni Om

Num Myoho Renge Kyo

Benedictine Monks chanting

I saw many different religions in many parts of the planet singing, praying and chanting for world peace.

These offerings of sound were all blending together in a harmony that became one vibration and the world shifted and were in perfect rhythm with the universe. The healing had begun.

As I listened, I could see a golden thread of light, the ultimate sound of silence, like the string on a baseball, spinning around and around the world. I had been seeing this image of the golden thread for a few months during my nightly meditations and prayers. I knew that it represented healing through unconditional love and spiritual development. I understood that everything in the Universe is one and that we are all connected; there is no separation. To kill another is to kill ourselves. That would also be a reason for Christ to die on the cross. He chose it, not only to give us eternal life by dying for us but also as an example to us that the only way to save ourselves is to surrender. Unconditional love is more powerful than hate, fear or death.

And, in an instant, I see Christ saying, "Father, into thy hands I commend my Spirit", as he breathed his last breath and died on the cross.

My entire body reacted and I felt Cleansed. Pure. Joyful. Ready for the next step in evolution.

About this time, my friend comes out of her study, looking energetic and radiant. "Are you ready to go?" she asks.

I truthfully needed a few minutes to get myself together, so I excused myself and went to the restroom. When I had regained my composure, I came out and we went to our session.

If you would like to sample some of these different songs, chants, and prayers, there are many options that can be found on Youtube. I have no intention of recommending one set of spiritual beliefs or practices over another. If you prefer to meditate or pray for peace according to other practices, please do. However you worship, or if you prefer to just listen to chants or music, that's OK. The vibration of sound does have an impact on all living things. What is important is that we create a world movement for changing the vibration of our planet so that we can live without violence.

The Buddhist chant that I learned to do while I was studying at the U of U is Num Myoho Renge Kyo. Here is a link where you can find it on Youtube: https://youtu.be/KfRcUpoPl7w

There are, of course, many, many more options. And I suspect that many of you may already have your favorites. And if you don't already have one, feel free to search for meditation, prayer, songs, and chants that bring you peace and please participate in helping yourself and our world with the healing that is long overdue.

OK. That's it.

Love and light,

Camille

Biography - Camille Amos

Camille is what most of us would call a late bloomer. She grew up in the '50s in a church that taught that women should remain at home and be mothers, taking care of their families. As a result of this thinking, she got married right out of high school and had two children. In order to help support her family, she worked a variety of low paying temporary positions. However, she quickly saw that if she wanted to be better paid, she would need to go back to school to get her BA degree. At university, she achieved a Bachelor's degree in Women's Studies and a Social Welfare Certificate, with the intention of working as a social worker primarily with battered women and children upon completion of her degree. Along the way, she also ended up getting a divorce.

Events at this time in her life led her to discover Buddhism. She found that the chanting calmed her soul. She also learned that if she listened, she could still hear the voices of her Angel guides whisper in her ear, the ones she had known as a child. Her life then took on new meaning in terms of spiritual growth and personal development.

On the other hand, when she finally completed her undergraduate studies, with her brand new social welfare certificate, her very first job was at the Hilton Hotel doing maintenance. She was good at it, she even enjoyed her job, it just wasn't what she spent all of that time studying for.

Finally, a position opened up as a psychiatric aide at a chronic mental health care unit. At last, something that required the skills she had acquired while she was studying. It was fascinating. She loved it; however, it was only for a limited amount of time. She had a six-month contract that could be renewed for an additional six months, but when the contract was up, there was no more work.

She had an opportunity to go to Brazil, where she earned her Master's degree in American Literature and then did Doctorate studies in Linguistics, with an emphasis on Teaching English as a Second Language.

While she was studying for her Master's and Ph.D., she started a business in order to support herself. She specialized in TESL for adult professionals in the community who needed to use English for personal or professional reasons. She also applied her social work skills to help them discover what kind of language they would need to realize their dreams, and focused their learning on those aspects of the language. The business grew through student referrals and she prospered. She also invited a partner to join her so that she could take on more students. Later, the business published, "The Big Mouth Gazette", a small English Language journal for teaching English. They also published, "Journalzinho Verde", a Portuguese language Journal written for children about the preservation of the environment.

Camille has also worked as an Independent Translator of documents and a variety of publications over the last 20 years.

Her work with TESL and the translation has been a labor of love to help people realize their dreams of studying or working abroad.

Camille is currently semi-retired. Her passions are personal growth, spiritual development, sustainable living and preservation of the environment. She is currently preparing her children's book, "Dream a Little Dream" for publication, the illustrations are in progress as this goes to press. And there are other stories in various stages of development.

She would like to thank DrG, for the invitation to participate in this project for Balboa Press/Hay House.

Also, thanks to Hay House Writer's Studio, making it possible for writers to get to know and support each other's work. And she would like to thank all of those along the way who have so willingly provided their support for her and her work.

Self-Mastery and Healing: A Journey of Unbecoming

By Riana Arendse

TO THE ONE WHO READS THIS

I say to you……

Welcome.

And I pose the question: Have you ever suspected that there is so much more to you, so much more to this?

Yes, you, the one who reads this now; who was so inclined and drawn to read this.

Know that this is for you. This is about you; your journey, your awakening, your healing, and your remembering. Your 'Unbecoming', your potential and yourself; as you Truly are.

This is how my journey began....

Imagine being a dolphin, thrown into a bowl with goldfish, and told to......Deal with It!

Well, that is how I would describe the feeling that imprisoned me - ever since I incarnated into this reality, which I, myself have chosen by the way.

And these would be the words I would hear many years later; words which finally resonated with how I was feeling...and THIS would later become...the beginning of My Spiritual Awakening.

My wake-up call, spiritual awakening and remembering had been a repetitive, incessant cycle of suffering and unwinding dissolution of what I was trying so hard to be – HAPPY.

In fact, for all of us, the awakening journey can be quite disastrous, eye-opening but necessary Gift, nonetheless.

This is a brief story of my Journey Home, my journey of Unbecoming, and the soul's persistent call to realize one's innate and true power: The journey of realizing who this is that has inhabited these bodies .... time and time again, life afterlife.

The mere fact that you are led to pick up this book and read it is an unconscious calling to you, perhaps to activate your Awakening, to catalyze your Healing and Unbecoming or to realize Who and What you Really are......

I will tell you this: No one who reads this will be left unchanged or at least a part of them will unbecome.

This is something I have been putting off for quite some time. Not out of fear or judgment, but as a necessary part of my journey; I have waited for the time when I intuitively feel inspired and called to share my journey of unbecoming...

I would briefly like to tell you my story of how I came to be a Healer and Spiritual Teacher...and how this came to be in existence. I would not ask you to go on this journey with me with an open heart if I did not first open my heart to you and share with you the story of how I got to where I am today.

Sometimes life must really, REALLY suck,
for you to want to end it and wake up.

I came into this reality, this incarnation, as a Severely empathic child. Ever since I can remember, I have always felt out of place, like I did not belong, and I never could understand why. And this started to become evident within my family relationship dynamics, and not long after that in my external reality, social circles and later, intimate relationships.

Unbeknownst to them, neither of my parents had healed their own emotional trauma before I was born. Despite being unaware of this, they still strived to do all they could to provide a good upbringing for my brother and me.

Those wonderful moments/memories with my family were so cherished, but in comparison to what followed; barely made a dent in the childhood I so wished to have.

Because I had incarnated into this reality as a Severely empathic being, I could sense things in people; their emotions, traumas and hurts, and take them as my own. My predominant extrasensory abilities were clairsentience, claircognizance and clairaudience. I just knew things about situations and people and didn't know how I knew. I was also able to feel spirit and receive messages through dreams, prophetic dreams as well. But for the most part, I didn't think I was special in any way. I was mostly quiet and shy, lacking self-esteem and confidence. I did not feel like a "Special little Girl". I found myself excelling at school, singing, music…. but never really understanding what the point of all of this was. All I knew was I needed to excel, I needed to show I was Special, to get validation and acknowledgment and ……love.

I felt so out of place.

The pain, inner conflict, and confusion that had begun so early on in my psyche, my being, had already taken a toll on me, and no one knew.

It's like I was born with a Spiritual System, Spiritual Inner Mechanism, that did not align with nor agree with the illusory worldview imposed upon me through Social Conditioning, traumatic experiences, and beliefs. I began sensing that much was not right in my life as well as within the world and started asking questions internally. This was a contemporaneous inner anomaly that plagued me since the day I was born; I just could not pinpoint it until my early adult life. This was the inner conflict I had been living with since my arrival.

The one persistent thought I would have as a child and all the way up to my adulthood was: "There has got to be so much more than this!?" Is this really it?? Really? I am just here to be miserable, sad and suffer?

I was only a child, but I felt as if I didn't belong – that I didn't really fit in anywhere. But that lonely feeling and isolation was nothing compared with what came next:

In an instant, I lost my entire childhood, and lost it over, and over, and over, again. And all events that followed mirrored this, with more intensity each time.

That instant right there is when I realized something had changed within me. That was the start of years of sexual and emotional abuse that I endured from ages eight up until my late teens. It was an incessant cycle of sexual abuse that became my inner hell.

What do you remember from your childhood? Do you remember having moments of being aware that something was changing for you, that the adults around you were inauthentic at times? For many, it can be earlier, it just depends on how early conditioning takes hold.

My parents didn't know a thing, I was not going to tell them all the years of unmentionable abuse I had endured. I was too ashamed, and I didn't think they would understand anyway, I didn't know if it was safe to say.

So, I had been holding all these secrets for years and nobody knew.

This was my reality.

And this would mirror my unconsciousness shadows with even more intensity as the years went by. I was living in a dark hole and wanted to die. I think this was my constant thought, as I didn't see a way out of this feeling of misery and depression.

I hated myself.

I had no idea how to love myself......

I had no idea what would make me happy and I also didn't know what my purpose was. As the years had gone by, my life mirrored back to me all that was unhealed and fractured within me, based on the law of attraction (that one attracts situations into one's life that is a match to the vibration or frequency you hold), and unbeknownst to me, my vibration was mostly based on lack of self-love, scarcity, self-judgment and lack of self-worth.

It appeared in the relationships I attracted into my reality: Relationships that perpetuated abuse, feelings of worthlessness, disapproval and emptiness. Little did I know that what I was really looking for, was MYSELF. And these relationships would reflect all the aspects within me that needed resolution and integration.

My career had taken off and I was working in the financial industry as a Bank Manager, however, this did not come easily for me; I had worked tirelessly and found myself overly stressed and unhappy. I had mistakenly thought if I could be financially successful, I would find contentment and happiness.

But I didn't.

I then began to question. I began to really seek answers. And for the first time in my life, out of desperation, I decided to seek a reading from a Psychic Medium. I was in my early twenties, and I can remember very clearly what she had said: "It might sound cliché, but your healing hands will lead you into the direction of healing.". And these words stuck with me.

A few days later, I had sat by my computer googling ways on how to stop smoking. And I had come across a site called "Healing Hands", where they advertised Hypnotherapy to stop smoking. Immediately, I saw the synchronicity in this, which took me back to what the Psychic had said (healing hands).

I then embarked on this journey to become a certified Hypnotherapist and NLP practitioner. This was the beginning of my healing journey and the uncovering of my purpose. This was the day when a little light was brought to my unconsciousness. I then began discarding my story, my pain, and really seeing the truth of the matter, and that there was a **Gift** inherent in the pain and suffering I had experienced. And the divine slowly provided me with downloads of information, a remembering of sorts. I remembered there and then, that I was the creator of my reality and that I am inherently a Powerful being and creator, and from that day forward I delved into everything that was dark within me and brought it back into wholeness. I welcomed all aspects of me that I (for so many years) have shunned and hated. I started healing myself and shifting my vibration and saw the gift in having to experience the things I experienced.

If there is a pain, a suffering that is deep, it will bring you back to itself until it is fully met.

Only by realizing the truth of things is everything set right. If we are lucky, we get disillusioned and traumatized so badly, that Life tends to help us to be emptied of that which is not real. We tend to wake up just a bit faster than the rest. The awakening comes directly from God source, to nudge its asleep part, known as you, awake. What is truly real? Why am I here? Why does life feel so empty? These very important questions are the beginning, the start, and the motivation for waking up out of illusion and suffering.

To me, spirituality is the willingness to completely fail, the willingness to completely be brought to your knees. It's the willingness to be courageous enough to completely face yourself, both light and dark aspects - even reaching a point of enlightenment still requires integration. That's why, although my clients and students think I've figured out something wonderful, I tell them all the time: my path was the path of struggle, a path of failure, internal death and absolute defeat. Everything I tried I failed at, even to this day life needed to show me huge lessons and dissolve many illusions, beliefs and hurts.

Consciousness was very Uncomfortable.

It doesn't feel good to see things about ourselves that we don't want to see. It doesn't feel good to recognize truths that we don't want to be true. And even though it didn't feel good at times, and I felt I was dying on the inside, my entire identity slipping away, all illusions revealing themselves; my Search for the Truth was always more important than any comfortability, joy or happiness.

In my most painful awakening in this life, I spent days and weeks being forced to accommodate and integrate all the things I didn't want and hated as part of myself. My mother being a witness could attest to this. There were moments I had wished I could go back to living an illusion in order to just find some relief...but the truest part of me knew, there was no turning back now, nor would I ever want to. I then had to completely accept all these parts as myself. This is the forced practice of self-love.

Life brought me straight to my knees in all its Power. There was nothing more I could hold on to, all that was left to do was just Let Go, Fall into the Abyss, into the Void. There was NOTHING left.

And even though I had failed many times, it didn't mean that the trying and effort didn't play an important role. The struggle did play a role. But it was instrumental because it got me to an end of that role. The Roles, false sense of self, masks, and personas all began to be discarded. I failed until it all was extinguished. I Danced the Dance and stripped myself naked until all was dissolved.

But at that moment of failure, that's when everything opens and reveals itself. These were the moments I knew a great shift had taken place. These were the moments I experienced true Liberation, true Surrender to a Higher Power that I knew came from within.

So, I encourage you to throw out the story of you! And see what lies behind the veil of your belief that you aren't it. The only thing that you have got to lose, is your unhappiness. You have yet to claim who and what we really are.

Your suffering is only found within your story; the mind-made story. When you are aligned within the present moment, you'll be able to access enormous power. Things such as trauma, false beliefs, and negativity limit your ability to access that inherent power. When you are in this state of illusion, you are experiencing fear -you are experiencing too much attachment to your mind and thoughts than being Present in the here and now. Life only seems to get worse when we are in a state of Resistance, yet we resist it in order to stop the negative feelings and situations from occurring, but all it does is make things worse. By focusing on what you don't want, you attract more of it – this indeed is the law of attraction.

To be liberated from this pain, anxiety, and powerlessness is to surrender to it completely. One needs to completely release the resistance and be present with the feeling itself, completely Present and Surrender to what is. Be in a state of Awareness and observe your thoughts that create these feelings and emotions. When you become aware of the thoughts, you will realize that you are not your thoughts; which are your illusory idea of yourself. Consequently, this is when the transformation occurs. The answer comes when we realize there is no problem at all, there never was—it is all simply resistance.

You can never be anything you are aware of, for they are only appearances within your consciousness, your psyche. Let go of your attachment to solutions and resolution, and accept what is; right here, right now, without resistance. Become aware most importantly of the triggers you have, these are the buttons that others press that seem to light up a negative emotion within us. These triggers are guiding posts as to what is still unhealed within us. AWARENESS is the first step. Master this!

To awareness, realizing that the whole thing is an illusion, is the greatest freedom. Then we start to see what is true. Your suffering is found only within your story; no story, no suffering. Then you will begin to see yourself Mirrored in all things and all people. Everyone literally is your mirror, and when I began to master being aware of this law, this fact, it instantly transformed my life. I knew I could use my encounters with others to pinpoint what triggers, traumas, blocks and limiting beliefs I still held within my being and then immediately shift them to the truth. Shift them to a higher vibration. And Replace them with something more positive, more in alignment with who I am.

Every perceivable situation and encounter that arises within your life is an opportunity for you to awaken, to transcend your humanity, and to realize your Self embodied as God.

Imagine getting to the absolute realization that you are more than just the constructs of your mind, and our attachment to it.

Imagine coming to the absolute realization of who this Reality is that is peering through your eyes and inhabiting your body.

This journey of awakening and enlightenment brings about this realization - (great doubt, great surrender, great death) and then ultimately the embodiment and expression of this realization.

So, starting right now, at this moment, I am asking you to become Source God/the Divine/the Universe. I am asking you to take your stand as the creator embodied as You, set the intention to awaken to the Truth of you.

At each, and every, moment, from here on out, have the intention to directly experience Truth, your true liberated Powerful Self.

After all, You, are a creator. Period.

The trick to truly Surrendering is to Surrender permanently, not just for the purpose of achieving a specific thing, person or situation, but a complete surrender of your life and everything you have ever come to know.

But I tell you this now - You will not incarnate into a higher vibration without work on your part. Nothing will solve all your problems and move you into a higher dimensional reality without you taking responsibility for your creation. What you have created is your responsibility and you are being guided now by the divine, the universe, God, who will support you as you grow and change and reclaim your manifestation as the Creator embodied as You.

If you believe that there is a God who is preventing you from having what you desire, that will be your experience. Whatever it is that you believe to be, will be so...this will be your manifestation. When we know the power that lies within us, we can truly begin to Unbecome, truly begin to heal, and truly return to the source of all that is – within.

And I say, go forth dear ones, go be a living example of Miracle Consciousness. Unveil the illusions, delusions, beliefs, projections, perceptions and completely Unbecome. This, in and of itself, is Liberating. This allows you to be a true vessel of divine love and divine grace.

Do you know who you are?

"When we surrender, we can experience our darkest moments as our greatest catalyst for transformation and expansion. Suffering will then cease, and a movement will be catalyzed.

Biography – Riana Arendse

Riana Arendse is known as the Spiritual Engineer; an internationally recognized healer, spiritual teacher, leader and Healing Catalyst. With a background in Psychology, NLP and Hypnotherapy, Riana's teachings are focused in the fields of Development, Self-Mastery, Direct Path method of Self Enquiry, and Spiritual Growth.

Riana illuminates the undivided nature of Life Consciousness with great clarity and compassion. Her events provide a direct and open-hearted invitation into the truth of who we are.

She is an energy conduit for Spirit, and her role is to transmit energetic words: Language of Light teachings and frequencies of new creation, designed to switch on more of our human DNA genetic codes, releasing traumas and instantly changing subconscious belief patterns; declaring our sovereignty and truly being liberated through Self Mastery, the Art of Surrender and Healing.

Riana later founded: "The Core Resolution Process™" - which was a combined modality she inevitably created, of which she used to Heal and Transform herself from years of conditioned beliefs, patterns, trauma and abuse; and could ultimately step into the light and truth of who she is. And so, it is her mission through her Teachings and Healings to help others awaken to their True Essence, True Power and those on the Path of Enlightenment.

Riana encourages us to strip away everything we know about ourselves, our lives, and Unbecome; in order to fully be aligned with the TRUTH of who we are. Riana's task as a Teacher, Healer and Transformation Catalyst, is not to answer your questions, but to question your answers. As it is your assumptions, beliefs, judgments and stories that distort your Perception and cause you to see separation where there is only Oneness and Completeness.

www.rianaarendse.com

https://www.facebook.com/Riana.Teachings/

Evolutionary Insight

* Names have been changed to protect the identity
of individuals. Pseudonym names are Ruth, Leah, Jimmy

By Orsika Julia

"Go to her. Ask her if it's okay for you to help her," I
heard the voice say.

"I'm sorry, WHAT?" I responded a bit befuddled.

I was in a hotel suite for a well-known transformational
speaker. This was my second time being asked to serve
after the conference hours. The first time was in Chicago,
Illinois. This time, we were in Atlanta, Georgia. I was
invited to be with the world changers, who accepted me
for who I am as a person.

They saw my value and I felt comfortable around the other servant leaders. Our mission and our purpose in alignment with our higher selves and each other. That's why we were all there.

"Seriously, just go, I'll guide you through it all." The voice was adamant that I walk over to Ruth*. I had a decision to make. Without any more hesitation I walked over to Ruth and quietly whispered with a slight bit of hesitation, *"Hey, I can feel all of the weight you're carrying in your brain. Would you be okay with it if I eased that a bit?"* *"Sure!"* She quickly responded.

With that, I began to listen to the Holy Spirit as it guided me through the *gook removal process*. As I removed the negative energy from her head, Ruth began breathing more deeply and purposefully. Her shoulders dropped, her mind felt lighter, and her energy increased.

"Now that you've taken away the negative. You must fill it with the light. Remember?" The voice was, once again, very clear in giving me specific instructions. I held my hands over her head and filled her head with the light from the Holy Spirit working through me.

It felt like time had stopped in those moments. I could have been there for five minutes or fifty years, the only way I was able to tell just how much time had passed was by taking inventory of the room itself. The food amount was still about the same. It appeared that there were team members still entering the suite. And the speaker had yet to arrive.

"Feel better?" I asked Ruth.

"Much."

I remembered thinking, *"cool, that was fun and easy!"* Then I heard the voice once again. It said to me, *"Now go over there to Leah* and do the same thing."* At this point, my confidence dropped, I dug my heels in and my response was meek: *"really? I just did what you asked, and now I have to do it again?"*

And even though I was pouting, I walked over to Leah and asked her if it would be okay for me to clear her. But on her, I felt the weight and tension were in her shoulders. Once again, I took the negative gook out of her and filled the void with the light of the Holy Spirit.

A week or so later, I got wind of some interesting news. Ruth* and Leah* good friends who had had a falling out. After their healing sessions, they were able to reconnect and come back together.

It's amazing to me how the Holy Spirit guided me, in a room full of people, to the two who needed healing the most. It was an amazing blessing to be chosen for this task in their lives. To be totally straightforward, I am 100% certain that *I* was not the reason they began healing their relationship.

From that moment on, as I meditate, I continue to ask for guidance from the Holy Spirit. I speak with God throughout my days and ask Him, *"What's next? How may I best serve you today?"* Sometimes the answer is clear. Sometimes the answer is silence. Either way, I do what I am called to do in the way I'm called to do it, every day.

I heal. I heal through social media posts. I heal through silent prayers for those who need it most. I heal by being whole.

Answering my calling wasn't the challenge. Understanding *why me* was more of a challenge. I felt unworthy. You read about healers in the Bible. They are the important ones. They are the ones we look up to for guidance and nurturing and love. How could I, who have been through divorces, abuse, and a multitude of not-so-great choices, be one of His chosen healers? How did I deserve such an honor? Then, I recall the countless stories in The Good Book that show us God's mercy and grace. I recall the stories of the underdogs being hand-picked by Jesus to be his apostles. My heart ignites with love and light at knowing He has had this plan on my life since before I was formed in my mother's womb. How powerful is that!

When I was younger, people came to me to nurture them and to give them hope. I had a friend in 2nd grade – Jimmy*. Since we attended a private school, we all wore uniforms. The *only* way to differentiate social class was by the shoes we wore. Jimmy's* mom was a single mom. (At that time, this was practically unheard of.) Scholarships were unavailable. She worked tirelessly to give her son and daughter a better education. Jimmy and his sister wore hand-me-downs and shoes that were quite worn out.

One day, Jimmy's* shoes were held together by duct tape. The kids made fun of him. They mocked him. They teased him. Basically, they tore him down. It completely hurt my soul to see him defeated. He couldn't help his socioeconomic status. Jimmy* was friendless, or so he thought. We were outside for recess when I noticed he was practically in tears from the cruelty of the others. At that moment, I had a choice to make (we *always* have a choice). I chose Jimmy*. I chose to be his friend despite mean kids saying we "liked" each other. It didn't matter. What mattered was that Jimmy* and I walked around the world together on that parking lot. What mattered was that Jimmy* was not alone. He knew someone cared for him. His spirit was uplifted – all because of a simple choice made to care about another human's heart.

Jimmy* was the *nicest* boy you'll ever meet; at least to me, he was. I knew him not only from school, but we also rode the bus together. We had time to really get to know each other daily on those bus rides. I have no idea where Jimmy* is today, but what I do know is that on that day, when he needed a friend the most, I answered God's calling to be that friend to him. I know that this is one of the endless examples in my life in which God has guided me to heal others and to shine His light.

Thinking back over my life, I clearly see how my gift and calling has always been to heal others. In just about every situation, I am capable to find the silver lining. I am capable to find that glimmer of hope to encourage people to move forward with their challenges. Sometimes, being the "silver lining girl" can be challenging. Sometimes, I also need someone to carry the weight of my cross for me. I mean, let's be honest here, even Jesus needed help carrying *his* cross. But, knowing that God is calling me to something greater than myself, allows for those insane heavyweights to be lifted more easily.

My calling, my gift, has been a natural part of who I am. I wasn't aware of it in my younger days. Since nurturing others was a natural way of life for me, I thought everyone did the same thing. But alas, I recognize that is not the case at all. I recognize, now, as an adult, that it takes a special soul to see past the outer shell and into the soul of another human being. It's a calling to not only see the soul but to be willing to help heal it as well. There are people who can see another's soul, but they direct themselves away from the hurt and the pain. And then there are those of us who lean into the hurt and the pain of others.

Of course, there's a fine line as to how much healers lean into another's hurt and pain. This fine line is called having boundaries. For those who feel others, boundaries can be an obscure thought, a farce reality. But it is critically important to understand boundaries. If boundaries are lacking, both the healer and the one receiving the healing can get stuck in the muck.

Thankfully, my calling as a healer didn't require any extra *work* on my behalf. It was my reality. I was shining God's light through all the stages of my life. Even during the darkest of times, His light shone. People felt connected to this light. They felt safe in this light.

Now that I've fully answered my calling, I am capable to intentionally guide others to their own healing. I have seen the healing of the spirit in clients in many parts of this great world. I will continue to answer my calling to heal one person at a time. The modality of my healing may change as I am guided, but the outcome will remain the same. People will heal through my allowing the Holy Spirit to work through me for the remainder of my time here on Earth. And I will continue to grow in His love toward a better understanding of humanity.

     * Names have been changed to protect the identity of individuals. Pseudonym names are Ruth, Leah, Jimmy

Biography – Orsika Julia

As the daughter and sister of refugees from Hungary, Orsika Julia always thought there was something unique about her. I mean, how many US-born children have Hungarian as their first language? She is one of the blessed few. (Of course, few is a relative term). Orsika grew up in the greater Chicago area, having lived in Illinois, Wisconsin, Michigan's Upper Peninsula, Louisiana, Oklahoma, Wyoming, and Texas. Currently, her soul is happiest in western Michigan with her three children and some fun animals.

Once she turned the leaf over of living in her fourth decade, Orsika realized just how unique she truly is. It was at this time that she became honest with herself and her calling. It was at this time when she realized the challenges in her life were leading to a higher purpose. It was at that point she stopped pouting and gave her life completely over to God. Because, without Him, her gift would not exist. Without Him, she would not be able to serve clients all over the world.

You see, God has called her to be a healer. Now, looking back, Orsika clearly sees throughout her life's events. However, now she is intentional with asking the Holy Spirit for guidance and discernment.

Pain builds up over the years of living life and struggling to let go of certain events. Therefore, healing takes time and effort. Having someone to hold your hand through this process, makes the walk a bit less lonely.

Finding the right healer for you is paramount. To set up a complimentary 15-minute consultation, you're invited to text Orsika on 616.730.2803.

Abundant Blessings to you!

The Self-Love Specialist Journey

By Karamjeet Kaur

I can do it! I did it, and I keep doing it! I kept me ALIVE and loving myself daily. Seventeen years ago, I was not the person I am today. I was someone who believed she has all possibilities, but over the years, trauma changed her from a possibility to a non-possibility personality. It started at age eight as I can remember (beginning of unwanted feeling), but it got worse after my sixteenth birthday. Being molested three times by a family friend/healer has led me to believe that I have no worth to my dad or family. I kept it to myself.

I was a typical teenager dreaming about being loved unconditionally, my true love fantasy, but bitter truth has made my dream to dust. It turned off my belief system of loving myself.

I feared so much of being touched. Yet I kept going, leading my life by simply ignoring the signs. I fell in love at nineteen years old, telling my boyfriend that I am a virgin and intend to be that way until I am legally married. He respected me. We were so innocent and respected each other's beliefs, but fate took us away from one another. I felt valued being with him which made me believe it is still good around. Then my world again got shaken because of family orthodox and negative thinking, I was forced to marry their choice. My first marriage only lasted two years. The absolute best thing that happened to me is having a beautiful daughter who became my strength. I decided to experience being a Mother to a soul even though I had not had my mom with me since I was five years old.

Going for a divorce was another nightmare where my mind turned me into a person who just wanted to end her life. I was twenty-four years old. I had a very bad belief that my life was going to be short because mom died young. So, this belief thought pattern embedded within me. Plus, I was pressured since young by the family with reminders of how perfect MY Mother was. They made it sound like I was her adopted child. I tried to keep my life happy, but I was very sad inside me. No one could see me. I felt unwanted and unloved. I had to prove my existence that I was a good daughter. I was tired of living to prove my whole life.

It never got better because I was a black sheep in the family. I was always reminded how great was my mother; it was sickening, to be honest. It is not that I hate it, I am proud to be my mom's daughter, but the way people said it to me made me feel like shit. Like a reminder that I came from hell or basically I was a street baby who does not have my dad or mom's DNA.

My family was against me when I agreed with my ex-husband to go through a divorce. I was blamed for everything: "you can't cook well; you can't take care of your daughter", but I wanted to study, and it was never encouraged by anyone. I was totally losing my battle of appreciating my existence.

My daughter was only two years old, yet I knew what it was like not having a mother and the mind was defeating me that I am worthless. I drove my tiny car in the fastest way to see if I can get hit. I was going through the worst moments, getting yelled at. There were so many issues and incidents that made me just want to end it. I was not even praying anymore, because I had lost my faith. Sometimes I felt to bring myself standing in the middle of a road of fast drivers and then I am gone.

I became lifeless. Only ONE thought was above the darkness, and that was my daughter. What changed my life, was the day I was detained at a local hospital for attempting to commit suicides. I have shared that story in my first book, **Truly Love Me**. When I was discharged from the hospital, I went back home and just surrendered my whole self to Divine Higher Power. I requested, *"please take me back now or please put me on a path that I can see a solution."* That was my turning point to receive the Voice that told me to "start 40 days" and "vegetarian." Only two words changed my whole perception of life. This was the beginning of my new destiny as the Self-Love Specialist. My life has changed 360 degrees.

****

The Voice has been guiding me to this day. It's been guiding me to believe in me and love myself. To trust life. I met a Spiritual Teacher after six months of hearing the Voice. I am grateful that He believes in my truth. I became his student for three years. I learned the world of mystical, miracles, magic and true love. He introduced me to Louise Hay after learning with him. I indulge myself with more knowledge of Loving myself.

With all the tools that were given to me, I applied them to myself. My life changed dramatically as documented in my book, **Truly Love Me**. I did my MBA to formulate modules on Loving self in a more comprehensive way so that I can reach people and students to love themselves. I am amazed by the miracles I see in people's lives as they practice Loving themselves after once having suicidal thoughts. Since 2012, after my graduation from MBA and going through the melding part of loving myself, I decided to share and empower people on loving themselves through my modules. I saw many people of all ages and genders experience suicidal thoughts, depression, loss, and anxiety. In the beginning, I did face certain setbacks of the following thoughts:

1) Will anyone believe what I do?
2) How will I do this, because I know the whole world needs to know self-love?

Questions keep arising, but my passion for sharing self-love never stops me from evolving into my true self. Writing my first book was the most inner healing experience in expressing the truth of my life. Over the years, I have been mocked, laughed at, criticized for my work, been looked down on and many things I face for being a Self-Love Specialist, but it never stops me. I am blessed to receive this gift that I can empower and inspire many out there by sharing more on self-love, playing an important part in humanity's grace.

Loving self or self-love is a realization of our self; being worthy and appreciating our existence. It slowly creates empowering belief energy of allowing all possible to happen in our life. I know what it is like to be in a total dark pit valley and it reaches the stage that you believe no one can help you. You feel you are not being understood. It creates the feeling You are not allowed to be true to self. You begin to feel outcasted, you feel like black gloom to people. You slowly move away. You feel the impossibility to create anything nice because You tried.

Today, generations are exposed to much easier ways in communication and more entertainment to allow the mind to wander. This is not wrong, but it creates a gap in the reality of love within oneself. Children are educated to be a perfectionist. The same mental program has been given in decades that strive to be best. High competition arises among these students and workers too.

The words 'perfectionist' and 'lack' have a major impact. When persons feel a lack of themselves (which generally, we all do because we always want to add something in life) it is really a very normal way of feeling it. Yet, when someone faces total discrimination of oneself, the lack-ness ability becomes more prominent. They will keep searching for people to fulfill their needs, materials things to satisfy their boredom or even suppress them to continue more in feeling lack.

The word lack has been holding a strong sense of power of feeling lack within us for decades. It is such a prominent word that creates a gap between individuals which separates us from being aware of our self-capability and strength. The gap has been growing larger over the years where it created fears in us to accept the belief of never enough in living our life. Due to that, many individuals keep looking for something to fill the 'lack-ness'. As one believes in a loving self, the gap lack-ness will cease in due time. It creates feeling fulfilling even its little to receive. It creates a positive understanding and appreciation, rather than the fear of belief in lack-ness.

As for 'perfectionist', it is fair to say that we are born to experience a perfect feeling in life. It's a natural tendency to feel perfect. Perfect comes in terms of being totally satisfied and fulfilled in oneself, but our perfectionist terms become about being the best of everything; making others feel lesser and accepted that they are not perfect as they are. I am not stating that being best of everything is wrong; honestly, it's great, but the mental and characteristic attributes such as being humble, down to earth, having the ability to allow failure to appear at times, must be accompanied.

I was carrying the feeling and belief daily for about twenty-eight years of my life that I am unwanted. All kinds of negative thoughts that are not aligned to love me. Once I decided to start the work of loving myself every day, gradually the confidence to lead life became easier for me. I faced many challenges over the years to become a loving person to myself, yet I did not give up because my feelings were changing. I felt it and I saw the impact on my life.

I, too, had the belief that life is not supposed to hard or rough. So, with this belief, I am expecting as I am loving myself daily, that my life is smooth sailing. Oh no, now this is where it gets tricky, the mind started fooling me. Hey, it's now worth all the love about you. To top that, whenever I face my past family or even some old friends, they can't believe that I have changed. My lifestyle and way of thinking have changed. It was another path to walk along with the change. Slowly, I began to understand the power of belief as it changes over the years. In my context, Life is never smooth sailing. As I change my belief that I am the ship that sails through the seas, I know there are days my ship sails smooth and there are days that are rough. It is my attitude and emotions that are my responsibility toward my journey as I sail my ship.

Previously I mentioned the Perfectionist term; well, this term refers to being unaccepting of facing challenges in life. We have been programmed that Life is smooth, but we were educated in schools on dealing with Life issues. These are the ingredients that mold the 'inner self tranquillity' of walking each day in life. The fact I am pointing out here is that we are responsible to our self the way we think about our self, what sort of idea we believe about our self, how connected are we to our inner Source, and to what extent do we understand our self.

Loving our self is the base foundation to build our convinced belief that we are perfect as we are, where we are. Whether you are facing debt in your life or you keep facing the same pattern of dejection in life, life is telling you to change your inner thought; the inner thought that is making it difficult to believe in a good way about money or feeling unwanted. If you are abused in your relationship, life is telling you to change your way of feeling that you are attracting the same experience because you are giving wrong signals from inside. Basically, any severe tragic moments you may face, even feeling bored to live life because nothing excites, it is only referring to your inner worth of how much you love you and your belief that you have been holding. The moment you change your feelings and belief thought pattern, is the moment you are in charge to create Your Life experience.

You will slowly understand that You are the ship and You are captain of the ship. Which way you sail, it's your responsibility to create the belief in you so you reach your destination easily and safely. I am going to repeat this fact again: DON'T GET TOO SMOOTHLY IN THINKING, YEEHA I GOT IT!! You've got to always be aware of what you're feeling and thinking all the time, and you've got to notice what is coming forward to you.

Sometimes (based on my experiences) the mind fools easily but not the feelings. If you feel something not good as you know to do good, listen to your Heart. Let it guide you. As you love yourself, you are increasing your connection to your body, your inner energy, they are always a part of you. I always recommend meditation daily for fifteen minutes to connect to the inner self and feel your breath. It is more than enough to know YOU.

Here are further methods that I always share at my free self-love short talks: The three main things I practice regularly in loving myself and I suggest you do it too, as follows:

1: Get a Mirror – Do your mirror work. Bless Louise Hay for this best method ever. Trust me, this is the basic need like we need to eat daily so we stay good. Mirror work is the same, you need to feed your energy of love. Say I love you every day and as many times you can. Say it while looking deeply into your eyes. Bring the feeling in you in every possible way.

2: Write positive affirmations daily. Write, "I love You" and, "I approve of You." As Louise Hay taught, it is the most powerful of affirmations. I can 100% guarantee that. Be creative with your words. Write a good story of yourself in your book of your life. You can change any good words and keep repeating the same for around six months and watch yourself in the world how you are representing yourself. See what you are attracting both good and bad. It begins with what you feel about you. So, writing affirmations helps you to be the person

You want to be. It's that simple. Write fifty times, the same repetitive sentences daily.

3: Get another book just for Gratitude. I say make your gratitude book as "The Aladdin Wish Book." It is amazingly powerful. Write minimum daily fifty things that you are grateful for in life. There are so many things to be grateful for in life. Be grateful for your home, car, your family, your career, food, and many things. You can repeat the same gratitude for writing daily. The more you appreciate what you have, the more you open to the universe for better to come. You can also write your wishes for the future by thanking it earlier. I can assure you that your Aladdin book will manifest your wish in time as you vibrate and love yourself truly.

With the three magical easy steps I have shared above, I can assure you, you will see Life as a Gift. You will realize that You are a Gift to be Alive. In that sense, you will not see the worst of you to end your life. You only wish to experience more magical and beautiful things. I do agree life is not always in a good sense, but through self-love, I learn it is not to Blame Life. In fact, to thank Life that keeps giving me the guidance to be better than yesterday. I make sure I appreciate the past where it gave me so much wisdom to understand my present.

My loving beings, we are here to experience our destiny through love. Love comes in many forms. The greatest form is our self, feel it in your very being, you will know slowly the true meaning of your Life here. As for me, my life is in my hands as I claimed it is. I know every second, I create as It comes. I still make mistakes, but I am so grateful to myself that I have never let it get me down. I note that everything that happens is always the door to make me feel the love of myself. I realize that I am always looking for light. Now the light Is with me and I am sharing the greatest belief key is our self. There is no way you will ever think of leaving earth without tasting the joy, love, creation that has much to offer. Love yourself for who you are. It is enough to move you to even greater heights than you can ever dream.

Signing off now. Thank you for reading. I sincerely appreciate you follow my suggestion. I would love to see more magic and miracles happening to you as we love our self. I love you as I love Me. Thank you.

Blessings of Love with all my heart.

Karamjeet Kaur, MBA, (Ph.D.), Self-Love Specialist Coach, Trainer, Consultant, Entrepreneur.

Biography – Karamjeet Kaur

Karamjeet Kaur, MBA(Hrm), (Ph.D.), self-love specialist, author, coach, certified trainer consultant, and director of Global Homeopathic Centre Sdn Bhd (GHC).

Karamjeet has a background of twenty years of working experience in local and multinational companies. She is currently pursuing her Ph.D. (Management) on Self-Love.

Karamjeet has been involved with social work since 2004. She owns a Wellness Centre that provides self-love, homeopathy, and other holistic treatments. Karamjeet focuses only on self-love empowerment, motivation self-help and belief thought patterns. She has been coaching and consulting patients and clients from all walks of life. She works with her business partner on creating wellness awareness of self-love with patients. She works in uplifting lives from suicidal thoughts patterns, depression, stress, young adult problems and many more.

She is married and has a beautiful young adult daughter who inspires Karamjeet every day. She finds that she is blessed to experience a second chance at life through many traumas. She is grateful to share her story to many out there.

She conducts free talks to teenagers and women on self-love for NGO's, Secondary Schools and Universities. Her new book titled, *"Truly Love Me"* was published in 2016 by Balboa Press, Hay House Division, USA.

Truly Love Me is Karamjeet's true story on understanding self-love and how it works in making life fabulous. Karamjeet is currently writing three more books about self-love, abundance and inspiring motivational quotes. Her aim is to wake up Self-Love in Humanity around the world.

Karamjeet writes for international online magazines and websites. She has been a co-host on radio online show, Empowering True Inner Self with Body Mind Radio, Michigan, USA. Her book, *Truly Love Me*, has been reviewed in local newspapers and she has been appeared in local Her World Magazine in 2017 as one of 40 inspirational women in Malaysia during Women's Day (March 8).

Karamjeet focuses on Self-Love work (Coaching or Training) as follows:

*Depression, Suicidal Thoughts Tendency, Anxiety, Panic Attacks, Lost loved ones, Addictions problems by Self-Love.

*Organizations Staff Awareness on Depression and Suicidal Thoughts Tendency by Self-Love.

*Schools, Colleges and Universities – Students Awareness on Depression and Suicidal Thoughts Tendency by Self-Love.

*Women Empowerment - Empower women of all walks by Self-Love.

Websites/blogs:

www.beingloveself.com

https://www.facebook.com/selflovespecialist/

https://bestselfmedia.com/author/karamjeet-kaur/

https://www.linkedin.com/in/karamjeet-kaur-2b7287131/

https://www.goodreads.com/author/show/14916638.Karamjeet_Kaur

www.lovelifehomeopathy.com

Twitter id: Karamjeet Kaur@Karam160399

Contact Self Love Specialist (Coach/Trainer) Karamjeet Kaur: Global Homeopathic Centre Sdn Bhd (Wellness Homeopathic Centre GHC)

14, Jalan USJ 11/3J, USJ 11

Subang Jaya

46320 Malaysia

Office: 03-80111550

Mobile: 0126952307

Email: kaurkaramjeet1976@gmail.com

ghc@live.com.my

Life as An Earth Angel

By Amanda Thomas

As a young girl, while growing up, I didn't understand feelings and wasn't in tune with my senses. We came out from England to live in Australia when I was five. I had a dysfunctional upbringing.

However, I have always emanated happiness no matter how bad my life got, with the feeling of comfort and happiness always inside me. I had an invisible friend who was a beautiful lady and I always felt wrapped in love, but she was invisible, so everyone thought that I talked to myself. She would often hold my hand and was the most beautiful "babysitter."

People have always been attracted to me, often have no idea why, and they say hello as if we are already friends. My aura is huge and filled with the purest love. Children also are drawn to me; it's the most uplifting feeling that gives me such a high and I love that I can give without anyone judging me. Conversely, this is very attractive to shadowy entities, so I must always be aware. I hear voices that warn me of anything potentially life-threatening; I used to fight that feeling, unsure if you are supposed to hear voices.

My senses grew when I became a teenager and I found it almost impossible to ground myself. As a result of my not being able to follow my better judgment, I got married at an early age to a demonic personality walking on earth; this man tried to destroy me.

What we must remember is that kindness requires patience and growth, love and empathy. Evil tendencies are very easy, no patience is needed. Around that time, my grandmother, who lived in England, passed away. Not long after she died, she paid a visit to my sister, who screamed so loud the whole house woke! My sister had been warned to be kind; nan had told her she had seen enough. My sister did go quieter.

Soon after that, I fell pregnant with the twins. It was a very difficult, traumatic pregnancy and as it progressed it became life-threatening. I saw that my invisible lady was right beside me, as it got so bad that I died. She was with me as I watched everything the doctors and nurses were doing to save my life. I still remember telling the doctors everything I saw; they had no words and were so humble as I told them they were the most amazing team

I had ever seen. The doctors told me I couldn't possibly have seen anything, yet I had been so close to them I could see the sweat on their faces.

When I think back, relationships have been the hardest, yet having a gift gave me the insight to know that each one was another stepping-stone. Something told me that all this was going to be useful with my gift, that I would understand real grief, empathy, raw emotion. Then, one day I realized people in need were purple! This realization took me to a new level, yet I knew I was ready and needed to start my journey into the spirit world.

I had a tarot card reading by a lady who told me I had to go and find my teacher, that I needed someone who was from the highest realm. I must say, I was a little scared. Well, I really don't remember where and when my teacher and I met, but I ended up with her, in a cabin. As we are going through my life events, I'm not scared. Listening intently, the next thing I know, someone has entered her body telling me the rules, telling me the paths that I would take would be devastating, that my healings were going to so very challenging. I was taught how to channel energy, how to use my third eye, how to meditate and still be totally functional. So, I'm excited, I'm using all this power, ahhh! Big lesson coming, I didn't remember how to close and protect myself; I can't reveal what happened, but I did run back to my teacher and we fixed the problem. I understood that having a beautiful gift meant to be very careful; evil and bad entities will try and take over you, they will sneak in. Since that day I have always protected myself. The fun things were blowing up microwaves, televisions, anything electrical, traffic lights, was so much fun practicing.

I AM AN EARTH ANGEL sent from the highest power of love.

I Began My Healing Practice in Earnest

The healings were exhausting, I learned limitations and the sharing of power; each person's needs were completely different, not one case was the same as the next. Then my sister diagnosed with Hepatitis B from within 6 weeks she was on life support in an induced coma. Doing well under the pressure, I gave up my business while my kids and I moved into the transplant units. She was dying and the doctors wanted to turn off the life-support machine; her brain had swelled and it was not looking good for her. It was the 6th of December, almost Christmas, so I took my little nephew's hand and we went to the Chapel. There was a book, so I started to write, pleading for this little boy to get his mum back. I filled it completely with love, then I signed it knowing that love miracles can happen.

Soon after, we were informed that a young man had lost his life, and the family had donated the gift of life. Wow! My sister received a liver transplant with no sign of rejection. She did so well and I thought we were finally going to be close, but it wasn't to be!

Healings Were Calling Me Again

My first case after my sister's transplant was for a family who needed answers due to a murder. When the tale was told to me, I thought, *I can't do this, to give them answers and earn their trust. To be able to give understanding, you must tell them things only they will know, and they don't like the fact I know, an understanding from them that I couldn't possibly know as I had never met them before.* This case was tragic; suffice to say I won't go into detail but I knew it was time to end this and give them closure. All the pieces were ready, but I needed another person because this case had taken its toll on me, so, I called in another young lady, who to this day has no recollection of what had happened. The healing was finally done and I never saw the family again.

My next healing was upon me very quickly: he was purple; in my head, I'm screaming, no way! Surely this can't be happening so soon. He went on to tell me his story; another tragedy. I put in place some people to meet to give him some peace. A man was at the hospital that day we turned up, he was retired, so a lot of amazing things happened on our journey, even people were offering us food and water on our travels, he couldn't understand what was happening and it was so beautiful, something he will never forget in his lifetime. We received many answers and he was incredibly grateful.

These are my greatest rewards; it is so calming the sense of peace, gratitude and validation. My life has been at risk many times, yet, somehow, I have always known I would be safe: my healings sometimes dealt with the worst criminals and I had to keep in mind we were not born bad. In those cases, the teaching of love is very difficult, especially when they have been beaten down to their lowest point (places that many never experience). Their survival instincts are magnified; I only hope the answers I have given them (in their quiet time they reflect and accept) are worth my time.

I would like to explain what I do in my healings and how it helps the person in need, with each person's needs completely different. I always have ambient music selections playing, as it is important for me to provide a safe, relaxed healing space. I make sure the first thing I do is ground my energy, protect and cleanse my body and aura, then I cleanse and protect the person. Whilst their aura is open, I usually get them to choose a cleansed crystal. I talk them through what I will do and guide them to take deep breaths. As I begin the healing, my hands become very hot and I remove any non-resonant energy, shaking it off with my hands. Next, I get them to close their eyes and then start on their crown chakra; when I first start, my hands get stuck on their body, opening and realigning their aura, whilst its open I fill them with love, this gives me a true reading on what's going on for them, and tells me if they are in their truth. After my hands become relaxed, I start blowing out all their negative energy; this sometimes gives me a choking response, depending on the person. When I know they are in a good space, I place my body close to them so they can feel me, as I wrap their body in the purest form of love. After they have had a reading, they will have five days of dreams; these dreams are put together, making sense at the end of the five days.

In some healings I have detected serious illness --- this is hard, how do you tell someone? I have decided to suggest going to a doctor for a check-up. When I sense death, I fill them with love so their passing may be quick with no pain. I struggle with this because a lot of family change toward me; they are hurt, I get that. All I can suggest is, make some beautiful memories.

One time, I took it upon myself to do a healing on a friend. I had always had a difficult time understanding this friend, it was always double-sided and she confused me. I did the healing and when I was done, I felt like a wreck. I had the shakes and felt very unwell. Friends saw me, they knew I wasn't OK and that I was struggling. When I got home, I went straight to bed. In the middle of the night, I woke with a pain in the center my back, so bad you couldn't touch me. There was a dark circle with many other marks on my back, so, I booked an appointment with the doctor, who said I had a spinal bleed. I had never had one before in my life and was so ill. I knew this was the consequence of using my gift for selfish reasons; it's a gift of healing, not one to abuse and I take full responsibility for what I had done. Floating between two worlds can be hard and sometimes I just take it for granted, but don't worry we still get punished to pull our heads in. I would highly recommend writing down your mistakes along the way as these are important lessons to pass on to others - not all of us need to learn the hard way. I love my gift, I embrace it, but I have also said, "I'm tired, I've had enough." It's beyond exhausting, draining and can have an impact on your health and wellbeing.

Ghost Tour Detours

One day, I had decided to go on a ghost tour with an empathic friend of mine who is highly sensitive. I wanted to completely open myself up and learn another experience in order to understand the history of what went on within the asylum. It was the middle of winter and extremely cold.

I soon discovered I was so very wrong to think it would be fun; the first building had me sobbing and completely broken as I physically felt what happened there in the past.

There were many sad things that night, and the saddest was the last room we went into; the shock treatment room --- the sense of something down the hall, it was strong, I kept saying to my friend can you feel him, can you smell it? We both came away from the tour completely wrecked.

The next day as we drove home neither of us spoke, both of us in our own thoughts. I cleansed myself when I got home, did a deep meditation, but I still didn't feel right. As I was cleaning my car, I heard, "duck!"; very loudly this voice was yelling. I ducked as this dark mass tried to attack me from behind. It was a vision I will never forget!

I have since returned several times to the asylum, there are spirits with a great amount of information; one man whom I connected with, Tom, told me he had ten very important things to tell me. This is the part of my gift I embrace; understanding the history of such a place of negative life experiences is healing and validating.

On another excursion, I booked a weekend away to Beechworth, which included an asylum ghost tour, plus extra paranormal. After the tour, a guide and I set up equipment that included a voice converter, a geo box, and other accessories. We experienced huge amounts of activity, off the scale readings; some good some bad, then we set up in the old theatre. Suddenly the guide asked, "is that you, Jack?" I knew it wasn't. I call, "James Clarence", (my father), the converter types, "Mandy", then goes on to say many other things to prove it's my Dad! He was standing so close to me, the love I felt was amazing, the most uplifting love.

I was there when my father had passed and am proud to say I loved him; the little girl loved him. I knew then, that weekend was meant to be! I never considered that anything would happen like this for me, and a confirmation that my life purpose has been to help heal and guide others.

Near Misses and Earth Angels

There are many lightworkers who have come into my life to save me. One such experience happened as I was driving my car into town. This day was a Sunday, so not much traffic on the road. Suddenly, I hear a voice say, "hit the brakes!" I reply with, "what for? there's nothing going on." Next, I hear, "hit the ^&*%$ brakes!" This time I listened and hit the brakes and as I did, a tire popped out of the car in front and was heading straight at my windscreen. In a split second, I'm working everything out; there was nowhere for me to go as there was an oncoming car from the other direction, it reversed itself and went completely the other way, within seconds, there was a lounge suit sitting in front of my car. The driver of the other vehicle had no idea what had just happened.

Another time, my family had sent me on a holiday to England to visit relatives, and while there I caught a cold. When I went to the doctor, he told me I had pneumonia and pleurisy; however, it was time to fly home as my holiday was over. My aunty gave me a sleeping pill, which I took. I felt very ill, my ears were hurting and it was difficult to breathe. The staff woke me in Dubai, called an ambulance and they took me to an airport surgery. By this stage, I was seriously unwell and they had contacted my family. I had no travel insurance because my family didn't get it for me, and the bill was $10,000. Soon after, a man walked in, asked what my bill was, paid the full amount and told them, "this girl needs to get home to her family." I was then put in a wheelchair and loaded onto a plane to go home. I tried to find this man before I boarded but I couldn't find him anywhere.

There have been so many similar experiences that have been life-threatening, I've always known everything will be fine. Experiences such as these are all part of my make-up; I learned true empathy, forgiveness, a love so pure you can't touch it, and patience.

Have I questioned my gift? Absolutely! When through pure exhaustion, and hearing so much devastation, my feelings of being not able to do any more traumatic healings, especially those that last more than six months. Helping others takes its toll on me sometimes, listening to real heartbreak, understanding real trauma, feeling their vibration, working out the truth from make-belief, stories getting extended. In the end, truth always shines through, and most people have that sense they don't have to hide their life from me. I've heard many bad things, things that have driven them to destruction. I've never had to advertise myself and what I do; people always have a way of finding me, some get very confused as to why I fall into their lives.

I was taught that before we can help others, we must first heal ourselves. Thus, making sure every day that I'm completely grounded is very important to me because even when I sleep things come to me.

On Relationships

This significant relationship is one that confused me. A very difficult person with no regard for others, life was all about her.

We met through a bingo hall and I remember thinking, *this girl has amazing qualities, but her behavior toward others and lack of regard and respect showed.*

We made friends, I was very ill waiting on spinal surgery, the pain was incredible, I was at my lowest point and my new friend was not great, depression had a hold of her. She was dysfunctional, in a bad relationship with a married man and her son was taking drugs. Gambling had become her 'out', a place where she didn't have to think about life. Having no job, gambling made her lose her flat and the downhill slope was approaching. She moved in with family; still gambling, this friend had no idea what I was or what I did for others, it was something I didn't think at that time she would even care.

Then one day, she was speaking very sure of herself, proceeding to tell me that she was so much better than everyone else. Her retort sent me spiraling and I thought, *omg, here we go, this is going to have a devastating result, karma is coming.*

And it did! Many bad things happened for a full year, nothing went her way, big things with lasting consequences, there was no time in her life for others, life was all about her. My patience has been pushed to the limit as over time I have been teaching her respect for others, training her a completely different way. These results are something she should be proud of and I am proud to call her my friend. Amazing tolerance was needed and it is hard to believe the girl she is today; she has respect, compassion, a full-time job, no gambling, cares for others. I knew it was all in there, I just had to guide her.

I have told her who I really am, needing her to understand why we would part ways, that there is always the next person waiting, and needing time to heal myself. It's been a struggle for her to understand, I can feel the hurt and repeatedly explain, this is how it works. I feel sad, too, for the norm seems so inviting, just being able to relax. I have enjoyed life, always something comes up, I have learned to just go with the flow but it's hard for people to understand that I can help more than one person at a time but they don't like to share, they never really understand why they feel the way they do.

When I was young, I couldn't understand why every male is attracted. It's unnerving when we don't see ourselves that way. Feeling like it's just the body we were put into, loving with so much passion, completely, which leaves doors open, so when we do get hurt, it impacts us on a whole different level.

Men have always felt threatened by my happiness, they have felt the need to hurt me to engage differently, to try to see or understand, how does she do this? In their minds, it becomes something of a challenge to destroy the happiness in me.

Falling in love for earth angels is extremely hard for us and I have learned to be honest, be straight upfront and tell them the truth; there are so many non-believers, you need to always be at peace with yourself before you take a man. Until we are at peace within us, we attract people who are damaged, they carry huge amounts of baggage, we sort it out, then they move on. We may never find true love, more to the point, we won't be able to keep them. Our work here on earth is not done, I hope one day someone who is like me, will find me.

Biography - Amanda Thomas

Amanda Thomas is a Carer for her five-year-old grandson. She has been an Earth Angel and Healer for over forty-five years and uses her gift of healing in many ways depending on each person's individual needs.

For more information and to connect with Amanda, find her on Facebook.

spent hours looking at different ways to do my planning and saving, and what worked for me years ago is not working for me now. I learned that balancing my energy and plans did not match, and I needed to realign with what I had put on autopilot years ago. Autopilot only works if your plans do not change, and I need to be more proactive in my choices.

Everyone is capable of LIAF. You take baby steps all the time, and do not get upset when you FAIL for the upset is the fear you have of Failing. Instead, you reset and remind yourself to get back on track the next day.

What steps can you take to tame your fear dragons?

Firstly, I thought about what I really wanted in life (which is allowing my intuition to be involved). It took time to make the decisions, and in some cases, I am still removing what our society has implanted in my brain as important and asking my heart and soul what is important to me. In my financial example, homeownership is a prime consideration. I know that I do not have the skills to do more than easy repairs around a house. I know that means I need to hire someone, whether it is a paid professional or a bartering type of activity with a friend, to do what I am not capable of doing. I also have to be reasonable as to whether I am not capable because I am not physically strong enough, or whether I just do not have the time to efficiently do it and it would be better to hire it out and have it done. I need to balance, based on a realistic view of me and my knowledge and capabilities, whether homeownership is right for me or whether it is a better plan for me to rent. It is not an easy choice to make, and it also may be a change in what I want as my circumstances change in the future. Right now, I have children living at home with me, and in the future, that may or may not be the case. Will my decision today be the same as one if I have no children still at home? Right now, I do not need to make my choice based on the far future, just far enough that it makes sense for now.

My second step took me to realize I needed to learn more. There are many competing ideas that go along with homeownership. Some financial planners and websites think it is great, and always good to have a physical asset. Others think renting is a better choice for many because it frees the time of care and maintenance so you can focus on other more important activities, which could include learning better investing techniques. In all the cases, and all the choices, learning from many different locations and concepts is important because there is rarely one right way to do anything. I needed to be able to have enough different opinions that I could sort through and make my own well-informed choice. We live in a world where we have the knowledge of all the ages of humanity at our fingertips. We all have the capability to take the time to learn.

My third step made me set a date where I would be done learning and ready to adjust to a new forward to success motion. With the knowledge of the world we have or can access, I know I could go down the rabbit

Navigating to my Niche

*Names changed to protect the privacy of individuals.

By Munira Zahabi

I believe that I have been placed on this earth for a reason. I have the unique ability to help people navigate to their niche. I believe that this is one of the jobs where my professional effectiveness is almost always narrowly measured by something that I need to find within my client.

As an earth angel, it is my duty to get people to believe in themselves. Everyone has the potential to do more than they think they can.

This is a humble attempt to tell my story as an earth angel. This opportunity has me taking a long look at the road I have traveled now I have reached my calling as *The Niche Navigator.*

The 'World Wide Web' was being televised like there is no tomorrow. K-mart was giving out Free CDs to connect to the internet and all of America was in a frenzy to purchase a computer and to get on the Internet. This was the gateway to the information.

I worked as a Teacher's Aide in an elementary school, and my job was to help students succeed in the classroom environment. Apart from the daily tasks, my job was to make my homeroom teacher's life simpler. The school district had invested in purchasing computers for all the classrooms. On the computer, we had two games, Solitaire and Snapdragon - an electronic coloring book. My homeroom teacher asked me to figure Snapdragon out, and after three days of playing with it, I felt like a master.

Pleased with my progress, I was later tasked with training the other aides. My teaching skills (I had been an elementary school teacher in Tanzania) came into play during this time and soon, I began to take on other roles in the school district. I loved imparting knowledge and it allowed me to thirst to seek new knowledge and opportunities. I believe the universe was preparing me for being an earth angel and this was the prep work I had to begin to obtain the title of, *The Niche Navigator.*

I worked for the school district for four years. I parted ways with this job when I enrolled in the six-month Pharmacy Technician program. It was a robust schedule with a lot to learn and memorize. My math skills were exemplary and in no time, I began to work after classes with my classmates to mentor them in the math portion of the class. I graduated with honors and received a "Mentor Student" award.

During this time, my love of technology grew. Microsoft had released Windows 3.1 to Windows 95 and to XP. I kept up with the upgrades on my personal computers and became well-versed in technology. It came easy to me whereas I saw others struggle. I speak about technology because it has played a large part in my life. This avenue was a methodology for me to reach to new heights when I met my friend Dave and all because of technology.

My children became well-versed with computers, games, and software and had scheduled times on the device and then at night after they retired, I searched the web for information. There was no sequence to the searches but information fascinated me. I frequented the chat rooms in Yahoo and soon befriended a man named Dave. In those days of "America online", the internet always hung up and most times I would hardly have more than ten minutes of browsing before getting cut off. He volunteered to fix it for me, and after much hesitation, I gave him my phone number and he helped me configure the modem.

Dave was as intrigued by me as I was with him. He was genuinely interested in my heritage, accent, culture, and celebrations. He was a drama major who now worked in IT with a prestigious firm. I could not understand how a person who had gone to school for one major was doing something completely different. This was a learning curve in the evolvement and transferable skills. A lesson that stayed with me and to this day use with my clients and I grow in my role as *The Niche Navigator.*

Contrary to others I met in the chat room, I found Dave to be a genuine individual who wanted to just talk. We shared our day and talked about other things. He motivated me to go to college by outlining all the classes that would enable me to learn to do what he was doing. He never asked me to meet him, and he was content with someone to talk to. This emphasized the importance of communication. I must note here that chatting with him improved my typing skills immensely.

He mentored me for a long time. He pushed me to pursue my master's degree and helped me with forms and proofread my college admission essay. He even walked me through the process again when it was time for my eldest daughter to apply for her college. He is a good friend who was genuine.

I often asked how I would repay him and his standard answer was, "pay it forward!"

During this time, I had graduated and was working as a Pharmacy Technician and Dave was instrumental in helping me find other avenues where I grew and I could enhance my skills. I often ran my ideas by him and he often encouraged me by saying, "you never know till you try it!"

I created and implemented programs in the pharmacy. One of which was to partner with other Pharmacy Technician training facilities to have pharmacy technician-interns complete their 120-hour internship under the supervision of a licensed pharmacist.

At any given time, we had at least three pharmacies technician-interns training in the pharmacy. As an earth angel, I was able to make an impact on at least two hundred individuals over the course of six years: most of them did not want to pursue this as a career but this was a means to an end and I was able to mentor them to also follow their dreams. Quite a few studied on and graduated as pharmacists, some of them just simply stayed in the profession, while some with entrepreneurial spirits started their own businesses after I ignited the fire within them. I worked in this role for over a decade. This position allowed me to grow in my career and it allowed me to pursue two Associate degrees, a Bachelor of Science in Business Management Information Systems and a master's degree in HealthCare Management.

Now that I had my master's degree, part of me wanted to move on. I applied for many positions and had several interviews. Then one day, out of the blue, I received a call and accepted a position. And just like that, my career as a Pharmacy technician came to an end. This was the job with my dream company and my boss, Carolyn, was awesome. I worked in Los Angeles and commuted a hundred miles one way to work. I did that for a month before finding a room for rent with a widow near the hospital. I stayed with her for four days, then went home on the weekends. I was able to take on this job away from home because my children were now all in college.

The position I took on was challenging. I had to gain the trust of the pharmacists and prove that the program we were implementing was truly a win-win situation for all three parties involved. I had to begin the task of hiring and training my team all under the scrutiny of the client. I grew, as did my territory. And within eighteen months of starting, not only did I cater to Los Angeles County, I was being sent to other hospitals, in other states as well.

This was a time where stand-alone hospitals were merging to form a system and systems were expanding rapidly. I was in the middle of Healthcare reform. I was solely responsible for thirty team-members that directly reported to me. Our team became a very well-oiled machine focused on finding and providing solutions, without hesitation and since we shared a common goal, it was imminent that I mirror the processes and procedures put into place with my other colleagues and their teams.

To keep up the growth, I began training some of my elite team-members to become decision-makers to make decisions in my absence. This was another milestone in my transformation as *The Niche Navigator*.

I was challenged in this job because my team members were not in one place. I had to find fun and effective ways to improve teamwork and identify their strengths and weaknesses. Each team member had a different challenge based on the hospital they were based out of and the state regulations. And meeting each challenge head-on was a growth factor for me. This, in turn, created a loyal team of high-performing team members who were personally invested in the success of the team, the region, and the company.

I love this role and built my employer's empire, but alas like all things, this too came to an end. I had worked with the best hospital systems in the nation and for five years proved that I was an effective leader, influencer, mentor and manager.

During my role with this company, I was sent to many leadership and other training and I often aspired to be the trainer and not the trainee. When this role came to an end, I was given the opportunity to take advantage of a job replacement agency and there I met people of all status, race, nationality who were in the same boat as me who were looking for the next position.

It is here that when I spoke to many people, I realized that most people were in a panic. Although the counselors asked them to choose the top ten companies they wanted to work for, they kept sending resumes willy-nilly. They needed a paycheck, and panic had set in.

I began speaking with my fellow job seekers and realized that they had no plan! They had no idea of skills they had acquired and when a job did post, they could not fathom applying for it because they were afraid.

At this time, I realized that at a young age, a child of eighteen is deemed to be an adult (some do this at an earlier age as well). This child goes to a learning institution and studies the ways of life or is sucked in the "survival mode" to find a job and survive. Many do climb up the ranks, but as life happens, they find a spouse and are constantly in a mode of working, caring, shopping and being in debt. It is when they are about 40ish and the children are leaving the house, they have worked in the same job for over a decade or two that they tend to wonder what their purpose is. Essentially, they have fallen out of love with the work they do.

What most adults fail to understand is that the job seeker, with a little discipline, can learn to seek the skills they have acquired and with a little thought process can qualify almost immediately to advance their careers by launching themselves as an entrepreneur but the problem was that they could not think outside the box. And if the entrepreneurial bug did bite some very lucky job seekers, they could not fathom starting a business because of, "what if?"

"What if the business was unsuccessful?"

"What if I can't secure a loan to start a business now that I am unemployed?"

"What if..."

"What if..."

This idea incubated within me and as I completed my time at the job placement agency, I became more aware of the fact that there was a need for someone who can help the job seekers navigate to their niche!

I began to seek a coach, a mentor, and an influencer and after countless searches on Google, Yahoo, I joined the John Maxwell Team. I fell in love with this man who taught confidence, credibility, and clarity. His curriculum allowed his team members to level up to bigger opportunities and give more impact.

The keywords were clarity and confidence. John allowed us to use his material to teach others and everyone who certified with his program came out Gung

Ho and were ready to change the world. The programs are incredible, as are the lessons. But to my utter disappointment, I realized that not all businesses wanted to have leadership training and there too I found something was missing.

I began noticing that some were doing very well, but there were some who were lost in the weeds. And to my luck, I was invited to a summit. A group of achievers gathered in the heart of New York City and it was then I realized that all of us were just "figuring it out".

I have become convinced of the following:

1. These people know that they will be in business someday, not just a business but a truly successful one.

2. These people have harbored the will to be an entrepreneur like a woman with a crush on her Jr. High sweetheart.

3. Whatever these people have learned thus far, has been an unconscious effort to prepare the entrepreneurial journey ahead.

4. Since there are so many who seek the same fruit, each of these people needs to create new standards of the rules that everyone has played by.

5. And most importantly, each person in the room needs to stand out from the crowd. They must be perceived as nothing less than *Special*.

6. Most importantly, each person in the room had to find a niche.

These revelations allowed me to get to the heart of the issue. It was like peeling an onion. In "peeling the onion" to these revelations, I achieved two goals. Firstly,

I was able to 'unsheathe' the layers of protection that I felt afraid of. I basically uncovered the FEAR I had. And secondly, I was able to establish the existence and extent of the problem itself. I had evolved to The Niche Navigator but I had to test my knowledge.

I invited my new friends to have a conversation with me. With some, a thirty-minute conversation turned into a two-hour discussion. I used five people as my subjects to test my theory. I helped each one look at what jobs they had held, the skills they had acquired and what they liked and disliked about their position.

Besides the others that I would like to brag about, here are a few I would like to share:

Lisa*, who had lost her job as an office manager in a dental office, wanted to teach leadership principles to her previous employers, mainly dentists. Secondly, she wasn't successful in securing an appointment with her previous boss. She was traveling to Italy, every five to six months to renovate her late grandmother's home that she had recently purchased. She was worried if she could make the trips next year because she was short on her money.

I asked her how many people she knew would like to travel to Italy.

Facts: Her grandma's house can easily sleep twelve; the house is about thirty minutes from Rome. It is not far from the vineyards. Everyone she spoke to about her trip, wished they could visit. Lisa knew the city, the culture, food, and the hot places to hang out and most importantly, the language.

I helped her understand that she sat on a goldmine. I had outlined and explained to her that she could expand her business and could conduct mastermind's while she was on an excursion. She looked at it from a different perspective and realized what I was telling her. In less than a year, she planned and organized four destination trips, an all ladies retreat, and a couple's retreat; she partnered with a Chiropractor to take some clients on a relaxing tour and another "just because" trip. She had found her Niche!

Anna* lost her husband and had to purchase a smaller place that needed to be remodeled. As she made changes to her new home, she realized that she had to go through the painful task of revamping her life. In her grief, she had to declutter and make room for the things she needed. This allowed her to go through her "things". Another realization that hit her was she needed to declutter her mind as well because a cluttered mind is restless and unfocused.

Facts: She belonged to a grieving group. People die each day. For grieving spouses, it is hard to declutter and let go of things, downsize and go through the painful process. Most grieving people need help and family members sometimes overwhelm them. Revamping one's life without the life partner could be heartbreaking.

I helped Anna understand that she had undergone a process. She had felt the pain of losing the love of her life. The pain of losing the home she had loved and lived a happy life. She had lived to find courage. She had written in her journal each day and she had that written testament that allowed her to share her pain with others. These facts helped her outline the common limiting mindsets that allow people to hold on to the things they own and prevent them from moving forward.

Janet* was a food sampler at a major grocery store. On the day I met her she was sampling cakes. One could tell she was not in a good mood and I heard her tell a few customers "Come back in ten minutes."

The cakes were in the freezer behind her and she had to warm them up in the oven to eat. I hovered around because I wanted a piece and my sixth sense kicked in sensing an opportunity.

I asked her if she was OK. She said, "Look, I know that was uncalled for but I need this job. The only thing is that I am giving out this cake and it's processed food!" She made a face and scowled. She made an emphasis on the word "processed" as if it were a bad word. "I make better cakes than these and mine are healthier. I just need this job to make ends meet."

"How are your cakes healthier?" I asked her. She rattled off some things. I should have been paying attention to her words but what I saw was a glow that seemed to emanate from within. My mentor would call it, "passion".

"Then how come you are not doing what you love?" I asked her.

"My mother said that there are too many bakeries in town and everyone is going healthy so no-one would eat my cupcakes!"

"Really? If everyone is going healthy shouldn't you make your cupcakes? How about I help you?"

"How would you help me?"

I introduced myself and told her she needed to follow my directions to the letter.

Facts: I ordered Janet's cupcakes. Delicious and Heavenly are two words that come to mind. She has five children each in a different class. She is friends with some of the teachers and parents in the school. She is a food taster at work - she can use the same concept at meetings in schools or small parties as well as give out cupcakes as a party favor.

I helped Janet understand that she has an avenue and can use the skills she is learning at her job to grow her business.

To cut a long story short, she has a standing order of cupcakes each day. Her cakes are sold in some stores. At the time I wrote this chapter. Janet is looking to sign a lease on a warehouse where she can grow her business. This could potentially change her life. She is still working for the store but only enough hours to keep her health insurance.

Over the past two decades, there has been a major paradigm shift and the coaching industry has exploded. There are many of us out there who want to coach and influence people but there are numerous coaching programs one can choose from. What is important is the *"you become clear once you overcome the fear!"*

The point of this story is to share with you that the niche you choose is within you. Haven't you been looking for something only to find it right in front of your face?

Finding a niche is not easy but persistence and personal growth will help you deliver your life's goals and ambitions. This persistence can be nourished and you can ensure that prosperity will follow. Only *you* are the captain of your ship.

Remind yourself that a good niche distinction is extremely important and a good niche has the direction that is only meant for you! The Starbucks story reminds us that creating niches is possible even when the economy is not doing very well. Your niche is quickly identifiable with your own personality, product and/or feature.

My job as an Earth angel is to build self-esteem and to understand my client; not only to teach the skills, technique and strategy, but also to help them understand the life lessons, and how they mastered hardship, how they handled and rebounded from failures and setback. How these helped them emotionally, as well as psychologically.

My job as an earth angel is to keep their niche in perspective, and not allow them to get distracted. The niche is merely a vehicle to understand their greater purpose in life. Most people get caught up in their ego and self-worth and are tied up in the outcome.

The whole point is that this journey is to navigate to their niche and despite these feelings, the most important thing to keep in mind is the outcome of the process.

As an earth angel, I know that each person is different. There is a different attitude, personality, response-ability, sensitivity and how they handle this inner challenge. My job is to understand and assess each client to achieve maximum effectiveness. Additionally, my job is to understand each person who crosses my path and help them navigate to their niche.

I grow with each person and I pray and hope that our time together is well spent as we embark on this journey together.

Biography – Munira Zahabi

Munira Zahabi, The Niche Navigator, is an author, speaker, influencer and entrepreneur from Chicago, IL. Through her business, she has influenced many people to navigate to their niche. She firmly believes that all people have a niche but are afraid to explore the deep, dark waters within themselves and sail a voyage through the raging waters to find it.

Munira's mission is to integrate the concept of niche-ology, business-ology, and confidence-ology. To learn more about Munira and her Niche, please click on to: www.Thenichenavigator.com

Co-author: - *She is the Ish, Journeys of Woman Hood.*

Co-author: - *Conversations with top Real Estate Investors, Volume 3.*

Master Interviewer:

https://www.youtube.com/results?search_query=munira%27s+musings

Munira's Musings:

https://www.facebook.com/pg/Munirasmusings/videos/?ref=page_internal

https://www.linkedin.com/in/muniraz/

https://munirazahabi360.com/

I Am Wholeness, Connected to Oneness and Free of Anything that Weighs Me Down

By Melissa Padilla

Our childhood is one of the most crucial times in our life. Everything we do has value and meaning regardless if we know it or not. As a child, I would do things that make sense to me now but may not have then. I'd pick up rocks, crystals, walk barefoot and I had the purest of hearts that most monks strive their entire lifetime to achieve. The things I've been through in life have always left me questioning, why me?

I had a fantastic intuition when I was thirteen years old. I remember living at my mom's boyfriend's house. We moved from 1010 Gold to his place. At the time, my family was going through a very tough time. The transition I was going through felt never-ending. I think we had been there four months when my grandmother died. I lived with my grandmother, Frances my entire childhood up until she passed away. I was extremely close to her; she was, and still will always be, my second mother.

When she passed, I felt my whole world come crashing down. She was one hell of a woman, they absolutely DO NOT 'make 'em like her no more'. I couldn't believe what she had been through in life at such a young age and that always played on my mind. After the services were over and a few months had passed, one night when I was in my bed sleeping, I woke up - but not fully - in this case I realized I was paralyzed. My brain was awake, I was aware that I couldn't move, and I was facing the wall. I kept telling myself to open my eyes and try to move. I couldn't move, it felt like it was impossible and that something must be wrong. The feeling I felt was as if something very heavy was on me. I couldn't breathe, anything you would think of to do at that moment, I couldn't do. I was, quite literally, fighting with all my might. After a few minutes which felt like an eternity, I finally broke free of it and was able to open my eyes, but I felt groggy and out of it. As I was opening my eyes, I felt and saw what appeared to be a reddish haze zoom off. I immediately started to pray. The next morning, I told my family and friends what had happened to me. I don't quite remember who told me this but they called it 'wrestling with demon's'. I thought about it every night for weeks. I realize now that being an empath and not knowing how to properly protect oneself from negative energy and vibrations, I was open to so much. It could have been Old Hag Syndrome which is caused by childhood trauma.

When I was eighteen, I became pregnant with my first child, her name was Keyana. I was beyond excited to be having a baby girl. The pregnancy went very well for the first five months. During my sixth month, I was very stressed because the father of my child was on probation. We lived together, and during this time his probation officer pulled us over, right when we pulled into our driveway. Two other officers joined him, and before we knew it, we had rifles pointed at us. The officers took him into custody because he had missed an appointment due to us moving into a new place. I was extremely stressed and upset during that month. I ended up having to move back in with my mother. Mind you, I had been previously going up and down stairs during the move. That same night, I ended up back at my mom's.

Deciding to go to bed early that night, I woke up that next morning in excruciating pain. I had been tossing and turning for hours before I realized something was wrong! I walked into my mom's room and woke her up. She told me to lay down next to her, and after a few minutes of laying down, I felt something warm between my legs. I got up quickly and with zero hesitation, I headed to the bathroom; sure enough, my water had broken. Keyana's legs were coming out of me. I screamed for my mom to call 911, I couldn't believe what was happening. I thought the smartest thing to do was to lay in the bath with warm water but the paramedics said to lay on the floor flat and hold the baby to my body. My mind was racing, my heart was racing, this just seemed unreal. I was in so much pain my body could barely handle what was happening to both of us. This was very painful to my body but most of all my heart. I was losing my precious baby at six months going on seven. She was my angel that I was so happy to be having but she was needed elsewhere. I remember being rushed to the hospital and my heart hurt in a way that I cannot describe. I soon blamed my ex-husband because he put me through so much. I couldn't move on from it. I ran so hard after that.

God blessed me with my daughter, Paris, about a year after. I carried Paris for seven months. I had to quickly make the decision to have her early because I developed Toxaemia; that means you and the baby could die, I know, scary right? Paris was such a fighter, she was only 2lbs 2 ounces when she was born. She had to stay in the NICU care for a couple of months before I could bring her home. I remember the first day I had her, the nurses put an IV in her forehead and she pulled it out; they said, "she's a feisty one", and didn't bother putting it back in because they had a close watch on her. Even at 4lbs when we took her home, she fitted into a men's size 12 shoe box, it was the cutest thing. She was so tiny I couldn't believe it. I finally gained my happiness back, I felt whole again, and I deserved to be a mother. After losing a child and then almost losing my life, and the second child's life again, making it through gave me the strength I never knew I had.

Speaking of strength, I feel I've been tested all my life and I knew there was something different about me. I attracted people and I innocently was oblivious to it because I am so big-hearted. I had my share of bad times too, don't get me wrong. I've made choices that I'm not proud of. I'm certain within myself because I've seen myself get through the hardest of times and I still am standing today. If I'm to be completely honest, there might have been a point in my life where I had been giving up on myself. I've been sick since I was eighteen; being diagnosed with diabetes and hearing there's no cure was one of the many things I've had to battle with. Being sickly, leaves you drained physically and emotionally, it's not something that you just prepare for. I never expected to develop more illnesses over time, I also never expected to end up addicted to prescription medications; the same medications I need to take to live. After divorcing my ex-husband, it put me into a deep depression and I thought something was wrong with me. I spent years wondering what I could've done, but I am here today to tell you I did nothing wrong. I was a victim of my own marriage. From when I lost my first child down to the divorce.

After years of deep, raw soul-searching, I finally found the real me. It all started with me seeing 11:11. Soon, I realized what my path is; these numbers I was seeing meant something more than just a google definition. These numbers changed my life. Over the years, I've met amazing people because of these numbers, and because of these numbers, I know my purpose. I spread love, peace, justice, and as an empath, that means the world to me. I'm able to teach and help lift lost souls like I once was. The moment I realized I was an empath, everything started to make sense.

I was always told by family and friends that I was uber-sensitive, but it's not that I'm more sensitive than others, it's that I feel so deeply and have always been in tune with myself. It wasn't others who needed to understand me, it was me who needed to understand myself. I truly found happiness when I came to the truth within myself. It's almost as if my twin flame is me. I've always had compassion towards others, even when I sensed the truth and things weren't always what they were painted out to be. Being an earth angel is more than being a kind person; it takes willpower, honesty, and most of all, faith. My faith in GOD is what has brought me through the trials and tribulations. I may have been through what most would call hell and back, but I know why now, and I live my life differently.

My perception is clearer, and my understanding of true unconditional love is stronger than ever. I chose to walk this path because it's the path that I know is meant for me. Finally, I am who I always was destined to be. Never give up on your hopes and aspirations, your higher self is always going to be there for you. Taking those steps to put yourself first in a way you never have before, and truly loving others is what being an earth angel for me is all about. Realizing your truth, owning it, and not letting anyone stop you from being you. I'm happy I am finally able to deal with the trauma I've been through. And I'm so thankful for coming to the truth of who I was always meant to be.

****

Raised Catholic, I was saved in a Baptist Church by my uncle. While I was young, I studied a little with Israelites, then woke up in 2012, when Jehovah's witnesses tried very hard to contact me and I started to go to Legacy Christian Church. I was following the New Thought metaphysical Community when I joined the 1111 movement. I couldn't make any decision, but I was growing. I felt isolated and was being cleansed, but because I have been diabetic for twenty years, I was taking 11 medications that were messing up my growth.

I believe it was God with me all along. I was led to my Herbal doctor in 2008, who I see now every month. Dr. Andrew Zeller believed in me so much when I had given up on myself. Around this time, a relationship with my friends and sister, whom I was very connected to, left my life and this was the last straw for me. Everyone in my life had abandoned me at one time or another. In some way, even the connection between my kids was off. I felt as if I had given to so many people, yet none of them were there for me. It's as if I had the plague and I felt like they all blamed me, even for their bad choices. I had made bad choices in my life, never put myself first and I hurt people I loved dearly; for that, I apologize♥.

I was running in complete survival mode and had no idea that you really shouldn't have so many people in your life; especially toxic people who take and never really give back, or not see what you do, only see what you don't do. I had become toxic, and when you're an empath, you feel so deeply yet if you don't shield or dissolve any cords, then you're being sucked dry. Can you imagine the state I was in? We all have cords of attachments to people we love, and when we don't remove them, we remain depleted and operating from that place. That is why I was so out of control. I don't blame myself, or anyone else, for not knowing.

****

One morning, my mom said, "1111 again Melissa, Angels are in the House". I lit up inside with a sense of knowing. I was guided to the 1111 movement; Jessica Regan took me under her wing and allowed me into the group, after that I seemed to become mute. I started to really go to another place. I not only started to see 1111, I was also seeing 444, 333, 555, 1234, 234, 1144, 1034, 1143, 666, 717, 818, 808, 888, 777, 999, 1133, 1033, and many more. I was led to so many healers and Spiritual beings, but I couldn't see or hear them. I had a knowing but just didn't trust it because I never really had anyone to show me the way. I was on a very low income to afford anyone who had truly understood what was going on. I followed free content daily, all day. I did a few workshops, such as a gratitude workshop, and I was being targeted left, right and center in my inbox. I took the bait and started to use $20 Mediums. I really was so ignorant of what I was letting into my life. I take full responsibility for all of it; innocently believing everything and everyone because at the core of who I am is a pure heart. As I stated earlier, as a child I had the purity that most monks strive their whole life to achieve. No, I'm no better than anyone else, I am who the creator created me to be and that is Missy, the one who loves everyone and has never really Judged other in a negative way. I accept the good, the beautiful, the bad, the ugly, and I have never had a racist bone in my body.

The traumas in my life did lead me to put so many walls up to the point that I stopped connecting. I felt like I abandoned myself, the inner child was screaming for true Love and Freedom. This was all because I was listening to everyone else and this includes family. I betrayed the one and only true love ❤ of my life: ME. Missy was trying to show me the way if only I would get out of the way and let the Essence guide me. I finally feel whole and connected to myself and am so very thankful for all the hard lessons that I have overcome.

Biography – Melissa Padilla

Melissa Padilla, a woman of God, loves her family dearly and wants nothing but the best from her spiritual journey. Melissa is the mother of two amazing children who call her, "honeybee."

Melissa was the Goddess who rescued Zeus; she collected honey from the bees, and Amalthea was the goat that gave Zeus milk. Zeus so worshiped Melissa, that he named the honeybees after her and the lemon balm that the bees favored for their sweet nectar; Melissa officinalis.

Zeus works with heavens angels that created the indigo children who have chosen to do remarkable things for the people, just like Esther in the Bible did for the Jewish people. The 144,000 will be anointed to bring many to the Light ❣

missybrandy77@yahoo.com

Woman to Woman

Geri Magee, Ph.D., aka DrG

There is no better time than now! As the world celebrated the 2nd International Women's Day on March 8, 2018, I found myself reflecting in amazement as I recalled all the women who inspired me to keep going, to keep trying, and to never give up. Many of my inspirational mentors are gone now, which left me with the realization that I am to 'take up the banner' and be an inspiration for women around the world. Over the following years, through my hard work and dedication to numerous national and international organizations, I gained great insight into various realms of cultural union and division. Thus, seeing diversity with open eyes and heart has encouraged me to keep going under adverse situations and ill health that I am overcoming in my own life.

It is with adoration that I have watched and participated in the multi-woman marches around the globe in honor of women over the previous two years. Being able to be a part of such a movement (for each of us to care for the other in compassion, love, sincerity and pride) has touched me to the depths of my heart. I have such great admiration for women around the world. I love that we have had a chance to have our voices heard. However, there are still many who do not know they have a voice or cannot speak up because of persecution due to societal norms.

As women, we need to continue to push forward. We have now shown the world we are bonded, and we can obtain unity of sisterhood no matter what, or who stands in our way. It does not mean you need to be radical; consider becoming a successful "agent of change" instead; not only for ourselves currently, but also for future generations, both female and male. I am feeling honored today in writing this chapter – a beautiful gift that the universe has given me to share my strength, wisdom and knowledge with the world – which has always been my personal successful endeavor.

I am a firm believer in the Law of Attraction. I truly enjoyed reading, **The Key to Living the Law of Attraction**, one of Jack Canfield's recent publications. I attended Jack's "One Day to Greatness" appearance in Seattle and welcomed him into my life in August 2017. I had grabbed the opportunity to attend the VIP luncheon and was able to introduce myself to Jack as *"his next business partner"*; needless to say, the room cracked up. So, there I was; on that journey alongside him, co-authoring SUCCESS BREAKTHROUGH'S with other successful individuals like myself.

As I went through life's journey from the unknown to the known, I watched (my family, friends, colleagues and acquaintances) and learned the lessons of life. However, the biggest lesson of all (that I observed and I continue to learn for myself) is the knowledge that knowing one's self is an essential part of success.

- How do I communicate?
- What are my likes/dislikes?
- What are my needs vs. my wants?
- How do I define this, and above all, be able to have the finesse to be successful in the world?
- How do I set boundaries as well as respect others' boundaries?
- How do I assert myself for the wellbeing of all?
- Do I respect and consider myself, as well as others who are around me?
- Do I practice on a spiritual path that brings me to the awakening of enlightenment, joy and happiness?
- Am I content that I can share my strengths with others on my life's path?

Many people look to the universe to find solace within the scientific and metaphysical world with amazement and awe. More questions we need to ask ourselves if we are to be complete individuals:

- Who am I as a sexual being?
- Do I take comfort and express myself to my partner?
- Is it in a healthy, open fashion to create that special intimate bond between two people?
- Do I talk about what arouses me and what does not?

• How have I developed my most intimate relationships with myself and others both personally and professionally?

These were questions I asked myself throughout my life's journey. My mentors have asked these of me as well, along that exuberant, bumpy, exhilarating and very eventful ride of life.

We are here for one another. The more we know ourselves, the more we grow and can share our lives with others. We may find that balance is not an easy feat. Growing up, my mother always said, *"well, life isn't fair."* True, I agree, but I also believe we have choices on our life's path to choose to see through various lenses. So, why not choose lenses that help you see the 'light at the end of the tunnel' as well as the variance of a colorful life? We are reflections of the life around us, so choose carefully and associate with those that keep you in that heart-and-mind frame. The lenses I have chosen aided me in surviving this confusing world. This alone keeps me essentially 'whole of heart' and open-minded. I choose to find solutions around me or within me. I continue to grow and advance (essentially) because my system is continuously growing, changing and adapting. And so, I must, if I want to keep the state of mind, body and soul that has allowed me to flourish in life itself.

Now, I am here to share a small part of my journey with you. From GED to Ph.D., the many lessons I have learned are not from a degree, but from a Godly/universal direction. However, especially in today's workforce, education is needed to move forward to sustain one's own life. I have been a mentor to both women and men throughout my two careers. I predominantly worked in an all-male environment that was, and still is, driven by men. This is where I learned fortitude and discernment. I learned about human nature (through ironic and comical ways of life) to help aid individuals, couples, families and businesses as a financial planner, banker, mentor and later as a therapist. This during my second major career shift in mid-life after completing most of my educational goals which gave me great insight.

Two-thirds of my clients were women who I educated and aided financially as well as therapeutically, in order to help them find freedom and be able to live a balanced and enjoyable life. I believe that by fortifying myself in advance through a male-dominated career. I was able to bring insight to many women and men as I worked and played in life. I found there is a karmic balance of fairness for one to keep going, learning and growing one's self in the miraculous balance of life.

As I traveled to cities, states/provinces and countries for either work or pleasure, I gained insight into the larger systemic world around me. I share this journey for those who wish to listen. As I have listened to those who have taught me in the past, now I bring that knowledge, love and compassion to the forefront of the current world we live in. Every day that passes, I continue to develop myself, bringing both the female and male aspects of my characteristic traits together with the multitude of 'hats' I wear. Each day is a new adventure in life, knowing one's self and sharing self with others. Even though many days may have been hard, I can look back into my own life and see the karmic balance.

It's amazing how we, as humans, can obtain so much knowledge from the world and universe around us, which keeps us sustaining the pressures of life and everyday challenges. But diversity is where we grow the most. I firmly believe that the 'school of hard knocks' is where our fortitude comes from as an individual and a participant in a very large, universal system. However, as I mentioned earlier, in today's world education is a must.

Education provides us with the foundation and basis of human development, insight into ourselves, as well as the various environments and their systems in which we participate daily, guiding us to interact with equilibrium bringing us to the homeostasis of the norm with which we engage with others. However, I believe there is relevance to bring all of one's authentic self to each of the variances, so we can remain whole and balanced in our individuality while participating personally and professionally in life.

Not everyone has an opportunity to attend school. In that case, then we learn by each encounter and endeavor we participate in. That's where we all diverge from others to become our own individual self; mind, body and soul once more.

Is education needed? ... many ask. My answer is, what have you learned from life? Life itself is an educational experience. Some have never sat in a classroom or had access to the internet or books for self-educating, but they still exist and grow. That's when the systemic community around them is one's own classroom of experiential teaching from society's norms and expectations.

Prior to my degrees, I learned by doing, watching and listening. Like many women did in my era, we all watched in awe the advancement of women in the global societal platform. Ironically, my own advancement came from helping others, to the benefit of myself, my family, my friends, my colleagues and my communities – both small and large – all with which I learned to be the kind, compassionate leader who I am. My goal was to educate myself while I was learning, to give as I was given, and to advance to the best of my ability.

Without my degrees, I was unable to advance to certain levels that I knew I was more than qualified for, based on my years of experience. I was 'ceilinged' out, continuously. By being one of the first women in the development of insurance products, policies, procedures and technological advancement of applications in various industries aided me in being able to feed my family, put a roof over our heads and have some luxuries in life that many women still cannot do in the societal demands and roles women must play/endure to survive. I developed myself through life with the aid of multiple communities, self-help and inspirational books, lectures and meetings, as well as various associations with people, businesses and organizations. All were predominantly symbiotic relationships in aiding each other in endeavors to reach the highest potential at each point and time in life.

Because of my personal need for insight, enlightenment and self-advancement for myself as an aide for all around me, I was granted a great opportunity to carry a message to others. I held onto that dearly precious gift that the universe bestowed on me. That gift of motherhood and grandmother-hood is one of the most precious gifts that I treasure. Being able to share the gift of knowledge through womanhood from childhood to adulthood is a blessing. I can now share these things with those who choose to be enlightened and are looking towards the advancement of themselves and their systems through the various messages I received from the universe – to help woman/mankind through understanding and utilization of the Universal Relationship Pyramid™ – primarily as a public speaker, educator and mentor. As I became ill, I found myself in bed for long periods of time. I had time for reflection. I used this basic pyramid tool as a thought process to aid me in the multitude of systems in which I participated in life to find balance and wholeness once more. I developed the Universal Relationship Pyramid™ theory years ago, prior to my dual degrees in Business Globalization/psychology - my bachelor's and Master in Systemic Therapy/Business Organization and a Ph.D. in Diversity. Along the way, I have added to it to help myself and others. All that participated in my life unknowingly helped aid in the development of the Universal Relationship Pyramid theory – a brick-by-brick breakdown formula to see where you are in your relationship with yourself, your higher power and others. Take it one day at a time.

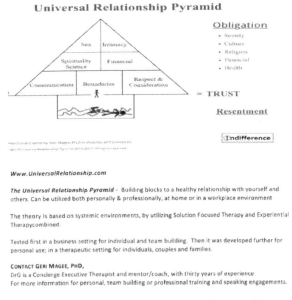

Diagram of the Universal Relationship Pyramid™

Geri Magee, Ph.D. is an honest, direct, and assertive woman whose life journey has helped both women and men from around the world achieve their potential. She has developed herself as a businesswoman/proprietor, a public speaker, educator, therapist/ mentor, contractor and employee for Fortune 500 companies. Throughout Geri's life, she has held many different roles; her best is that of a single mother. Her success is not something she did alone but with the help of the community around her. Geri started as a Financial and Estate Planner at age 23. She later made a midlife career shift after earning a bachelor's and master's degree both in Business Globalization/ Organization Development and Systemic Therapy, and a Ph.D. in Diversity. Geri believes you don't need to be aggressive with people. She has observed in her life that aiding others multiplies success. Geri helps others to stand up and work together to achieve their goals. That's true teamwork in motion! Leaving someone on the sidelines was never her 'cup of tea'. She looks for the potential of every individual around her and couples it with her own to make the world better. In 1992, Geri first started her career in the insurance industry, and become an expert in the field of asset allocations and preservation of assets within two years. She worked mainly with women to develop secure investment strategies for financial freedom. At that time, she was one of the few licensed women in the industry. Top banking and insurance companies recruited her to develop their insurance and financial divisions. It wasn't easy for women in the industry to accomplish, but her 29 years of successfully creating multiple products and programs aided her in working and contracting for major companies such as Allstate, AAA, Hartford, Safeco, NY Life and Mass Mutual, managing multiple locations simultaneously through multi-tasking and adaptability. Geri has received several 'Woman of the Year' awards both professionally and personally. She has a background as a p/t radio host and has been on Good Morning America, in Sacramento magazine and is a member and multiple-award winner of IWLA.

Geri specializes in solution-focused and experiential therapy practices, coupled with degrees in business organization. She owned two practices in Western and Eastern Washington until 2014. Then she became ill but is now beating all odds and statistics. Geri remains healthy and positive about life, an inspiration to all who meet her. Geri created the "Universal Relationship Pyramid" with theories she used for over twenty years in both profit and non-profit organizations. She states, *"utilizing the 'Universal Relationship Pyramid' is easy to do if you break the pyramid down brick by brick. You can create the life you want. First by understanding who you are and secondly by how you choose to react and resolve the various situations and environments around you. After ten sessions most clients never return, successfully resolving situations in their own systemic world. Clients/Patients learn multiple skillsets from the Universal Relationship Pyramid to move from the unknown into the known."*

The Joys of
Getting to Know Oneself

A chapter from **Warrior Women with Angel Wings: Illuminate your Joy** by Dr. Sundi Sturgeon ©2018.

Geri Magee, Ph.D., aka DrG

As a single mother at the age of eighteen and again at twenty-three, surviving in the eighties and nineties, I was lucky to myself in the lucrative field of finance, insurance, and banking. There were not many women in this field at that time. The most popular woman, other than myself was Suzi Orman from the Bay Area, California, and I was in Sacramento. Many women had just breached into banking in the seventies and early eighties. It was not an easy time for any woman because of a wide-held belief in an industry run by men that we woman couldn't do math.

What I believe made the female population sustain themselves, besides being well-educated in the field of math, was that we were very good at developing and sustaining relationships.

There was so much trial and error throughout is one of the first main women in the North-eastern part of California that it could become daunting at times. Much of the trial and error was based on, and from, my innate intuitive nature that made things work to pave the way for future generations of both men and women in insurance and the financial sales market.

By the mid-nineties, my nerves were a wreck. I had already had a panic attack which I thought was a heart attack, so did my colleagues. I was rushed to the ER; it was by far one of the scariest experiences of my life. I began to take much better care of myself; I taught aqua aerobics, yoga, I meditated and followed a spiritual routine every day. I had dabbled in some hobbies in my early twenties but never committed to any of them. I was a bartender in San Francisco with my first daughter and made good money working at the Bank Exchange; which was a night club. I find that humorous since I later in life went to work for the finance and banking industry.

Finding a balance between both the financial world and the spiritual world was one of the greatest gifts I could have received from my higher power, bringing universal love and harmony. After the third small panic attack, a friend had me go see a psychic; it was after my stepfather (Dad) had passed away. At that time, I was thirty-one, and it was a unique experience because I hadn't ever had a reading before.

I was waiting in her office in Fair Oaks, California. Both friends said they did not tell her anything about me. They both had chipped in, to give me a one-and-a-half-hour session. It was about twenty minutes before the door opened; remotely, which I thought was the coolest thing to see.

Just before I entered, a toy in the toy box that was in the corner of her waiting room started to play, "Frere Jacques," a song my father who just passed, my mother and grandmother (now deceased as well) would sing to me and my siblings. I thought *wow, how strange*; I was sitting there for twenty minutes and no sound before that. As I began to walk across the room, this very famous psychic looked up and said, *"Oh, your father is with you."* I just blinked, thinking my friends must have said something to her. As I sat down, she then said, *"So is your grandmother, sweety, by the way."* I got chills. Now the one thing I never told anyone at this time in my life was how close I felt to my grandmother. The day she died she came to visit me right after her heart attack. She said, *"You will be fine, sweety."*

(Now, the thing I have never been known to do was to sit quietly, ever, in my whole life. But you better believe it, I did; throughout this whole reading. To this day, I don't think that I have sat that still in all my life. This includes my post-op coma in 2005, where I pretty much died on the table and was in ICU for ten days; the nurses stated, *"You would move your feet to the music, in tune, every time the Ellen DeGeneres daily show came on, also you would laugh at the appropriate times."* So, the nurse's station decided they would turn it on each day from that day on. When I awoke, they told me I had to start walking, so I got up and did. The nurse had to catch up to me with a second gown, stating, *"I said you had to get up and walk, I didn't mean now.* " My statement back was, well all I heard was, *"You have to walk, so I did. ").*

I veered off the timeline to explain how active I always am.

The psychic continued to talk to me about my family members who were angels, about why they were visiting me today with the words I have remembered the most. There were other messages from a few others, but the two most important to my life rang through the loudest. (This gift also took the edge off my panic disorder. However, it did not take away the anxiety and fear of having another panic attack or the worldly stresses of single motherhood and many other things that we experience in daily life). She did go on to tell me that by the age of thirty-five, I will come into my own abilities. I did not want to hear this. One; because of my religious beliefs at the time. And two; because my dreams were nightmares, usually. Which, by the way, I did come to know and accept, and my angelic messages over time started around the age of thirty-five.

What only very few people knew prior to the time of my father passing; I dreamed he was reaching for the phone and had a heart attack before he could answer it. I did many things to prevent this from happening; as soon as I awoke startled by my dream; including making my dad promised me he would go to the doctor.

Two weeks later; as I arrived home from a long trip from Sacramento to San Francisco and back again on the same day; I found out my father had a heart attack. I called immediately, he said, *"I remembered your dream, pulled over at a fast-food stop because of chest pains and collapsed asking for help.*" I was crying as he told me the story and my heart and soul were happy to hear he was in the hospital. Three hours later, a family friend called to inform me he had passed away. To this day, I know both are my guiding angels amongst others who watch over me and my family.

When growing up, I was always told by my grandmother (Hungarian) that I was a natural healer and seer; as was she, my mother, and now my children.

I predominately worked with women, and occasionally their husbands, as a licensed massage therapist.

One day, I became ill from a patient who did not have a cold, but a tremendous amount of turmoil in her life and that was eating her up from the inside out. That's when I learned about transference.

Whoosh was a big lesson to learn about. I was sick for two weeks until I was able to get my chakras cleared by two powerful friends; along weeks of self-healing

I started Reiki level one to block negative energy, at both my healing friends' insistence. The reason, they said, was primarily because of both careers I was working in, Reiki is gravely needed.

A few years later, I finished Reiki Level Two to help others. I found there are many people who don't enjoy physical touch.

Much later in life, I finalized level three: Reiki Master, while in Japan. This journey brought me to a stillness inside, of myself and the realization of time.

Japan was a very memorable spiritual journey for me to experience.

Being raised Jewish on my mother's side, and strict Catholic on father's side, made my spiritual journey to date an interesting step-by-step incline and learning process to my higher power and the knowledge of universal love.

My grandmother taught me about palmistry and the third eye (she did not call it that) of insight and wisdom. My mom loved astronomy, so with them, as well as my other strong-willed female family members, they all were my guides in my life.

My educational process went along the same line as my spiritual growth.

I took my education from a GED graduate at the age of seventeen in New York state. Miscellaneous classes in nursing/physician assistant, CNA and other licenses and certification in insurance, finance/estates and senior advisor throughout my young adult life.

Then my BA in Business Globalization (Law)/Psychology, double major, in my 30's. I then received my MA in Systemic Therapy, and minor in Organizational Development in my 40s, and finally PhD in Diversity and Divination In my 50's.

I found each step and each turn of events my way, through resilience and patience, love of self and others, and most importantly, the very important lesson of universal love for each other.

So, the gift my friends gave me was one that was immeasurable to me in the human form. However, one fully beautiful, of the souls' life and universal love of guidance from our angels, who watch over us, day and night. As my life went on, and I continued to work in the financial field, I also studied to become a licensed massage therapist and Reiki Master to balance out my life (and to provide extra income).

The balance I achieved is what started me on my beautiful spiritual, knowledgeable, journey through my life. As I am praying you have begun in your life.

Calling all Earth Angels, Healers and White Lighters: Awaken to Your Senses

Chapter title: "Sense-a-tional Readings"
Written for **Reading Between the Signs** by Jill
Rhiannon ©2019

Geri Magee, Ph.D., aka DrG

I have listened to the wise of my elder earth angels since I was very young. Women and men who have helped mold me into being the person I am today, and I continue to grow with the earth angels that are around me in my present days; to all these people I say: *"Thank You."*

Now, the reason for starting my chapter this way is I believe all of us are earth angels who transgress and learn each day by sharing and modeling each other. Now, if you ponder the question, *"how am I an earth angel"(?)*, your answer will come in time. Many people have asked me who I think is an earth angel and how they can become one? My response is, you already are, and if you are caring enough to ask, the signs will come to you. I was so giddy at being asked to participate in co-authoring this book with Jill and the many other esteemed authors.

I love reading between the signs that my angels have given me. Not only do I receive visually, but they have also used audible ways of communicating with me. And since I love food, they have even given me signs through tasting. It is one of the most powerful ones because in just a moment your mood can change. The sense of smell is more powerful than you realize for better or worse. Both are needed for learning lessons in life. Some have asked, *"How is that so?"*. I have designed a great workshop called, "Sense-a-tional Journaling." It is a guide with your angels and mother earth, utilizing aromatherapies.

Well, I adore all of my angelic guides and for me, I see them as having a great sense of humor in the way the messages have transgressed and been relayed to me; which have left me laughing many times over the years, as well as on numerous occasions, left me crying.

So, now I go on to share some of the messages so that you too can begin to see the signs in your life; and discover that to be guided by angelic love is a blessing to us, earthbound angels.

My visual messages tend to be my most memorable, due to the impact that is ingrained from the subconscious portion of the brain. Generally, audible messages are mainly recalled in dreams, or in an emergent situation which triggers the 'fight or flight' response.

Now, tactile messages recall from the amygdala; which is in the medial portion of the brain. Our Spirit-guides reach us by utilizing various universal and environmental tactics to relay the message that we need to know. So, we must be on the lookout for all, and that begins by knowing yourself in mind, body and soul so we can see, hear, and feel the various signs that are being sent to oneself.

Besides the sense of smell/taste, four of my favorite universal/angelic signs I love to share are:

First Sign

Tactile had been an interesting message to many from me, usually about another person. For instance, the one I recalled while writing this. My daughter and I were on the outs, I told her I am not going to call unless she apologized for speaking to me the way she had. Well, three weeks went by and I didn't hear from her. As I was closing the light and was blowing out the Halloween candles around the house and not feeling good; I had a stuffed-up nose, and my ear hurt so I used my grandma's remedy; olive oil warmed on a cotton ball in my ears, I could hear nothing. It always worked for me before and even on my kids. I believe a lot has to do with hearing your own archaic rhythm being heard.

That night, suddenly, I felt and heard a very slight whisper, even my cheeks hairs stood up while a light breeze went past me, and the whisper was my daughter's name. Now, I have had this happen so many times before in my life that I know to listen to it immediately. I put what was in my hands down, reached for my cell phone, and remembered I am not speaking to her; she should apologize, and I don't believe texting is talking, it can be misconstrued. But I know I had to hear from her when this happened.

So, I decided to text. "Hi sweetie, its mom; my weird thing happened just now, so I need to check on you is everything ok?" The returned text, "Hi Mom, no I am not good I am in the ER." My text was, "OMG I will call."

She said: "No! I have a tube down my throat, so I can't talk." We lived in different states, so I couldn't just hop in a car and drive to her. She did live with her father and she had her friends who were able to help, and her boyfriend there in ER with her. She checked in with me the next day, and her boyfriend kindly sent me a text once she was released and home safely. As you can see, when you sense or feel this sign on any of your sensory intake, remember to stop, take a deep breath, relax and then take the actions that are needed for you to be aware of what that sign is telling you; about your own needs, or that of someone else's.

Second sign

Just knowing every fiber of your being and all senses fall into place is all it takes to know your angels are telling you it is right, and you can feel it through your five senses into your sixth sense.

It was during Christmas shopping; my dearest friend and I had promised gifts for the kids only, no gifts for each other. However, I was in Barnes and Noble and I saw the book, "How to Talk to Your Angels." I loved reading this book, she had flipped through it a few weeks ago, and she seemed very interested in what it had to say while reading. It was on sale, and every fiber of my being was telling me to get this for her. So, of course, I decided to buy it for her since she was hosting Christmas that year. That was my great resounding sign for not following through on the gift-giving promise this year.

My kids and I showed up for Christmas dinner at her place. I told her, "I broke my oath, I found a gift that I thought you would love," and I apologized. She became so excited and said, "I am so glad you did because I found you a gift too and I think you will love it too." So, like two happy little girls who each got a surprise, we ripped open our gifts.

I could tell it was a VHS, and later she told me she could tell it was a book. Well, it turned out I gave her the book on talking to your angels and she gave me the VHS that the authors did for demonstrating how to talk to your angels. We both cracked up. After eating, she was telling me how she was in the checkout line, like myself at Barnes and Noble; the second she saw the VHS, she had to get one for herself as well as for me. She too struggled over our vow; gifts for the kids only and the quick, final decision, the cashier had called, "next," so she grabbed it. We laughed like little girls, and to this day we both love to tell this story.

Third Sign

Now, as for the audible messages; which have been many, but the one that is most memorable was in a very small bagel shop. I was in line buying some bagels and my lunch. I had had something on my mind and I was procrastinating about what to do. Something came up in a conversation that I was overhearing from the two people behind me; they were speaking loud and clearly, and I was listening intently. My turn was up to pay. After paying, I turned to thank the two people behind me and no one was there. I asked the cashier if he saw the two people leave, he said no, but that he saw them as well. It had been nearly three seconds that my eyes were averted to pay the bill and to see the small shop. Plus, they would have to have asked me to move my briefcase to get past me. The cashier and I also looked in the bathroom to try and find where these two people went. We finally gave up, but he remembered seeing them there, and he remembered the conversation, as I did, but no one was next in line. To this day it has me dumbfounded.

Fourth Sign

I had an issue weighing on my mind for two days and I was not sure what to do about it regarding a friendship. I had deliberated on it over and over for two days. As I was driving home from my children's school, I stopped at the corner lot, and right there was a huge billboard sign that had the answer on it. I felt it in my gut, heart, and Soul. I was stopped only by a moment at the light, but I could not believe what I had just read so I made various turns to get back to the corner to appease my mind on what I had just read; even though the rest of my body was content on the topic, my mind was not. I reached the same point again at the stoplight, and about five minutes have passed. I look up to the billboard and it said, "Got Milk?" I was flabbergasted at seeing the sign that just answered this question with a, 'Got Milk' sign. By the way, it reminded me that I had to get milk on my way home, my son alone would drink a gallon a day.

I drove away thinking, wow that is crazy. I stopped at the local store to pick up the milk that the angelic messages reminded me about, and there was the friend in question. With the questioned already answered, I was able to comfortably speak with my dear friend and set my boundary politely and reasonably, which in turn she did the same, and our friendship did not end over something I had deliberated over for two days; to be resolved by a billboard sign.

Another visual sign I have used since childhood is license plate readings. We used to play it on family rides for fun. I have read some of the funniest informative license plates or bumper stickers, with peculiar, funny and enlightening heavenly angelic messages driven by earth angels. A recent bumper sticker said, "zoom-zoom" my daughter's phrase I read on a license plate last week. The next day she called; I wasn't at all surprised. Being a grandmother my new favorite to always see is "baby on board;" a definite reminder to all that small earth angels are present; the message being to be a safe driver.

My most favorite license plate memory goes back to age thirty-two. I had been stuck in a two-hour traffic jam from construction workers and of course an accident that delayed everyone trying to get to work that morning. The manager of my dress shop and consignments store was unable to get to work to open shop. It was our first day carrying homecoming and prom dresses to help keep the business afloat following 9/11. We converted the bridal room into a ball gown area with dresses that fit plus-size young women. I had traveled to Las Vegas in the spring that year to speak to various high-end designers to look at and discuss the various shapes and sizes. We took all orders for plus-size to smaller sizes. This was the first time in the industry. Plus-size young women either had to wear a bridesmaid dress, handmade, or hand-me-down. I helped create positive change within the garment industry, because of my eldest daughter's and many other's needs of healing from bullying for plus-size teens. I was determined that my first-born earth angel was to blossom as a beautiful woman; as we should guide all our young "Women Warriors with Wings."

The sample dresses that arrived were amazing. We had worked hard on setting up the dress shop. I and a few other local business owners wanted to help with the sorrow of the nation and our local community after 9/11. We wanted to bring a breath of fresh air to saddening global change that had impacted all. The local top ten radio stations did free advertising for the businesses that participated in the event. We had the local limo company donate the driving to the dance from the store that will be broadcast on "Good Day Sacramento" the next morning. Included was the local Mary Kay representative, and Hair Salons volunteered to do the winner and her entourages hair for the night's gala event. None of us were to know the impact this would have, but we all prayed for a positive one. Other local communities were doing similar events. But our store was the hub central for dresses.

The day of the drawing was to be held on our first opening of the gala dresses display. I found myself amid this traffic jam not moving at all. I was receiving calls letting me know how many people were outside; the stress surmounted minute by minute. To distract me from the time, I looked at the stores, the people, and finally the license plates. I started with the furthest one I could read and worked my way over near me, much as I did as a youth when playing the family car ride game.

It took me a while to make out what the borders around the plate of the car in front of me said; I finally got it:

People Are Good

Work Is Terrific

Life is Wonderful

I said this over and over and finally got it, I mean I really got it! inside to the point it changed everything immediately and for the rest of my life, which includes all that are in my life near or far, known or unknown.

The cars started to move when I finally read the actual license plate; it said, "ATTUD" =Attitude! OMG!!! I made it to the store waving and apologizing as I drove to the back of the stores to open shop; mothers and daughters lined up. My daughter and employees thought by now I should have lost my mind to the point they stopped calling me because I was so stressed on their last call. I asked them not to say a word, to prep to open, as I ran around looking for paper and mumbling to myself. Finally finding a marker and paper I called a quick pep rally in the back. I pinned the paper to the wall and told them all the above affirmation is our new motto. I had us all say it three times and they all started to see, feel, and believe it. It was the highest sales we ever had in the business that day.

The store opened, and we had our highest sales ever. Everyone had a great time laughing, joking, and some whispers and teasing with glee as the plus-size young women tried on their dress that fit them beautifully. All the while hearing the thinner young women complain that the dresses don't fit as we worked hard pinning them back and picking out their dresses. All happy with their purchases when they came to pick them up; we had our own alteration staff on hand to make sure nips and tucks were perfect for each girl for that special magical guided night.

The earth angel owner and driver of the car that bore the license plate "ATTUD," probably had no idea of what a life-changing effect they had on me, and most likely others who have taken the time to read in passing. But more importantly on a community and the world that needed saving, that spread throughout the darkest of nights of the earth angels brightest light, that we will all get through this together.

As for the winner of the dress, well that's another beautiful story of earth angels coming together to bring light to another earth angel's life; a true Cinderella story to be told another day.

Many blessings on your new path to knowing yourself as an earth angel and discovering what other heavenly angels are trying to convey to you.

With much love,

Dr. Geri Magee aka DrG. Theorist of the "Universal Relationship Pyramid.

You Are Your Own Sunshine

Chapter from: **Warrior Women with Angel Wings: Gleaning the Positive from the Negative** by Dr. Sundi Sturgeon ©2019.

Geri Magee, Ph.D., aka DrG

Do you know that famous children's song, "You Are My Sunshine?" My parents sang this song to me as a child. I now sing it to my own children and grandchildren. I was caught many times by my kids (when they were younger) singing it to myself in the mirror while getting ready for work. The kids would make fun of me while singing the song in the car on the way to school.

What they did not know at the time, as a single parent raising three kids plus their friends (who came to visit or predominantly lived at my home), was that I was an example of how I wanted my own life to be. I had to be happy for everyone else to be happy, or so I thought.

Twenty-three years now of working on my co-dependency issues in relationships, I discovered I can't make anyone else feel what they do or do not want to feel.

I also found out the reason kids loved to come to my home was that I chose to be happy and had created a positive, safe environment for all, including at times the parents of the children who came over to visit. I went to bed singing the Sunshine song and I woke up singing the Sunshine song. I realize now, looking back, that I created my own sunshine, every day.

I know it wasn't an easy thing to do, day-to-day and yes, I had my moments of deep sorrow and pain, as everyone does in one's life journey. However, I took the opportunity to learn from those times, to make sure I did not repeat the underlying issues and yes, my goal each day was to find the "silver lining" in the cloud throughout most of my unhappy moments. What did I learn from that experience, what did I want to leave behind from that moment in time, and what did I want to take ahead for the future? What I learned from each lesson was to not 'repeat the bad' to see what lesson I learned. However, to also hold onto what was good from the situation and the outcome of it.

As I progressed through life, I kept manifesting this trait of my personality in that I truly *became* my *own sunshine*. As I grew, friends, neighbors and family members would nickname me Sunshine, and I realized that others could see me as a person who brings spiritual light into the world.

Recently, I had someone very close to me say: "Why do you always have to be so happy even if shit goes wrong?" As I looked at that person, I truthfully and whole-heartedly said: "Not all of us have to wear the darkest parts of their heart and soul on their face and in their body language." I choose to show the world (or at least Geri's world; those who come and go from my daily life's journey) that I know what hardship is. However, I do not believe it is beneficial to show it all the time especially professionally, believing the old adage's; "leave your worries at home" and, "leave your work at the office," have helped me many times.

I survived extremely difficult circumstances in my life; however, I still choose to live by demonstrating the beauty of it all and my heart and soul radiate from the inside out. That's how gleaning helps me find the beauty and spirit in all things with my own mind, body and soul. I believe that is how many earth angel's life and continue to show their light to themselves and others.

I had an experience recently; someone close to me whom I care for considerably was going through multiple situations. His life events came crashing down around him; one wave after another impacted his work, continued education, home life and of course, himself. This person snapped at me and said: "Why are you always so happy and cheerful, are you putting on a fake cheerful face?" I looked and said: "No, I am not. When you have time, I will be glad to sit with you to hear all of what is going on and I will be more than happy to share with you how I get through each day."

I do not believe I am a farce; authentic, I am true to myself and others. All of us earth angels and energy healers have a light that shines brightly. I believe most have this power, it's just that some people have their light more deeply hidden than others.

Earth angels and energy healers who work on themselves daily, shine their light brightly. Generally, we know each other even before speaking. We easily find each other in our daily lives, exchanging pure energy to keep each other going. Recharging each other without ever needing to physically touch or verbally connect. When we do connect, almost everyone can see the surge of energy go up and around us, some witnessing they can feel their own energy go up as well. These are pure evident traits of an earth angel and energy healer which make each of us shine brightly.

So, I ask you: Are You an Earth Angel or Energy Healer? If so, what type? What behaviors and traits do I see in myself that has kept me going throughout the adversities in my life that help me pick up the pieces and keep going to share my light with others?

These are great questions to ask yourself in order to generate the light you have inside and in gleaning your own life. I do believe the light of positivity shines inside all of us, we just need to get out of the basement of gunk and muck. Push away from the negative and discomfiting intentions of what others' want you to do or feel. Only YOU can make yourself feel and choose to be proactive rather than reactive in life!

I have learned over the years in my codependent recovery that I need to stop for fifteen minutes to disconnect from the negativity, place myself in a safe space, do an internal check-up and look at what is going on inside and around me. I then ask myself: "Who is causing this impact that dampens my light, trying to sabotage me from being the person I choose and want to be?". Also: "Who can aide me during this time of need?". Especially while trying to put life's little puzzle pieces back together again. I ask myself, "when I go back into the toxic environment, what do I hope to change within myself? If possible, can I do action versus reaction, utilizing my inner consciousness and spirit collectively for the best outcome?". "If I cannot change anything in my current system, is there a way to find the resource I need?". "If resources aren't available, what would be the healthiest exit strategy?".

My primary goal is to be as authentic and truthful to myself as possible. I can see myself start to glean, and as I do my light comes out and I try to mindful of those around me when I start this miraculous change in my environment. I ask myself: "How are others in my system reacting to this healthy change I decided to create?".

My best advice is to empower yourself with self-love! Believe me, I know it's not always easy, it can be very painful too. It does feel so much better being aware of who you truly are! The first few steps are hard I know. However, you will see your 'shine' immediately start to come through once you leave the negativity behind you.

Throughout my fifty-plus years of life, I have learned that by choosing to live and view my life in a positive way, each day as often as I can, that it is the innate nature in which I have utilized the law of attraction.

A few weeks later, I saw this person (mentioned above in my life) look happy for the first time in a very long while. I said: "Wow! What happened in your life that is so great?". The person said: "How can you tell?" My answer: "It is so obvious on your face, in your body language and I can see your light. How have you been picking up the pieces through all the negativity?" I was told of their past day's events from waking up to moving forward through a super stressful week; further stating: "No matter what is going around me, I am going to find the good in this day! As I have been, from since we last spoke." They believed they could do it and so, they did!

Not only am I a firm believer in my own life's law of attraction, but I am also witnessing so many others who have accepted their true inner gifts. I have had the privilege to watch as each of them day-by-day makes progress to enlighten themselves and take notice of the power of positivity. They are already sharing it with others, as I am with you as you read this chapter. By watching the law of attraction unfold in another's life journey and by personally experiencing the law of attraction in my own life seeing from my own eyes, my heart and soul feel this immense energy that comes out when applying these actions on my journey. It is one I would never take for granted (or allow another to stand in the way of), my light shining in order to aid others, for that is what I believe keeps each of us earth angels and energy healers going, each and every day as we pass each other in silence or in personal encounters.

Now, for the person I spoke of earlier, when they began to glean their own truth and authenticity, others became aware and witnessed their transformation. Doors started to open for them in multiple areas of their life. I am privileged to be a witness to their transformation since they are so important to me. I firmly believe positivity draws positivity and the things that we fret about become life-changing events for us as time goes by.

My friend was able to save his job, move to another division and reap the rewards to allow his soul to shine through, whilst gleaning through the negativity. I must mention; during this time, he made it through multiple events of departmental reorganization, management changes, job changes, layoffs, family member illnesses and passing, plus a lot more than he had on his plate.

While making these personal changes he had no idea how many lives he was able to impact before leaving his division. Now, as a friend, I know this is work-in-progress and just baby steps toward having a happy, fulfilling life. As I still grow, beginning from many years ago, now, they must, too. It is a beautiful gift to be a part of someone else's life, nonetheless.

Here are just a few 'tools' I was shown that have helped me to navigate the experiences of my life, both personally as well as professionally.

1. Write down a list of all the people you love in your world. Now, please do this before proceeding further in this chapter. If, at this moment, you are unable to write for any reason, just think of the people you love.

2. Were you stuck in my theory? Writing things down can help clarify things in your mind and help toward a solution.

3. Look at your reflection in a mirror (your whole self) and say to each part of yourself: "I Love You." This can be a very difficult exercise. A therapist told me to do this years ago, it has been successful for myself as well as for others.

4. Now, on your list of loved ones at step 1, what number were you? If you were not there, write your name at the top of the list. Trust me, I did not have myself on my list either a year ago. I now keep this in my bathroom, where I can see it each day. A part of a guiding light's resource is to look at oneself from the inside out.

So, now to share my story of how I learned to glean. There have been several times in my life when I have been in the deepest part of my 'very dark basement of muck' with confusion, regret, stagnation, the list goes on in "Geri's World." Many came to rescue me and many times God/Universe made it clear I need to rescue myself; no one else can do it. How I started my first realization of this was in my early thirties. I was going through so many of life's changes, constantly feeling I was being hit by wave after wave like I was going to drown in a deep-sea and the more 'waves of life' that hit me the more I felt I was drowning into my dark matter.

I finally went to seek professional help. My therapist was wonderful. I didn't know how valuable each was in my times of need when I was younger. In one case; after a few sessions my counselor told me: "I want you to go home and write three good things that happen to you each day." "Ok sure, why not," I thought. I didn't know how hard this would be!

A few weeks went by; I was even more depressed then than when I had started therapy! I had not written *one* thing down. Then one day, I was outside in my backyard thinking, "wow this will never work! Nothing will work; ever work! Why am I even alive?". The infamous question many ask our self at some point in life, during a depressing time. The sun was beaming as I cried and sat on the stoop in the backyard. I had been sitting in my dulled life and having a terrible day (like always, thinking it will never get better!) when suddenly, I saw a ladybug land on the screen of the back door. After some time, I reached over and had him walk on my hand, just enjoying that moment, with the sun keeping me warm. Then he lifted his wings and flew away.

That night, I lay in bed in my 'stinking' thinking mode, trying to think, "what good came of the day?" Suddenly, the ladybug crossed my mind. So, I sat up, turned on the light and wrote: "A Lady Bug!" on a blank piece of paper and then fell fast asleep. I had a therapy appointment the next morning. I went to it with my piece of paper in hand, still saddened that I did not have three things written down. I gave the piece of paper to my therapist and sat down. She opened it and said, "that's wonderful!" I thought I was going to get chastised, as I had felt leaving the past few appointments; this time for not finding and writing more down. However, looking back, that was *me* creating that feeling of chastisement inside myself, not her. In addition, looking back, she was the first one in my life at that time who said something positive to me. It had been months not hearing a positive word from someone else. I now realize I said nothing positive to myself, either.

So, I left her office, ran some errands and went home glum as usual. As I fell asleep, I thought, "oh, what good came out of today?" Immediately, I wrote the good things that happened that day:

1. I wanted to attend my appointment and I showed up. (Accountability).

2. I remembered my paper to show her and to tell her about the ladybug. I felt proud that I had finally actually written something down. (Accountability).

3. I didn't cry when I got home.

4. I ate something I liked, relaxed while I ate. Truthfully not really wanting to eat, but I had brought home a great dish. Afterward, I lay in bed thinking, "wow, today was a great day!" I sang: "You are My Sunshine" to myself before bed.

The next day, I awoke to feel much better. Much more alive than I had felt in a long time. I didn't question it; I just sprang up and started my day as usual. When I had my next therapy appointment, I brought in a small notebook, there were a few pages of things I thought were positive and the things I accomplished. I continued counseling for a few more sessions. I then realized I didn't feel the need to go to therapy every week, so we moved it to every two, then once a month. Eventually, I was stable on my own once again, feeling bright and sunshiny inside and once again outside as well; others noticed.

Now I display my light and positive energy as often as I can, both on the inside as well as the outside. I review my progress when things are looking grim. Now I can glean through the negative, each, and every, time. Many factors can pile up and it does become difficult. So, when I have an obstacle these days, I go right back to my journal, write the good things each day and then look at the progress I have made over each week. Peace and rational thinking begin to kick in gear, solutions show up and I move forward just like everyone else.

I chose to share this story because none of us ever feel great every day and there are times in each of our lives when life just bogs us down, we feel unhappy, discontented feelings and non-fulfillment of life's purpose for oneself.

There are resources out there to be found if you are in need or want to have help. One happens to be my theory: "The Universal Relationship Pyramid," a block-by-block building instruction to finding a healthy relationship with oneself and others.

In my theory, there is a basement of gunk and muck. Here we can become stagnant, stuck and unhappy. We eventually, after a time, build up resentment and feel as if we are dying or already dead inside. This is a clear sign we need to filtrate the negativity from ourselves. Once we do that, then the positivity can flow back through us. I am a firm believer in this and try to practice the stepping blocks each day in "Geri's World."

By the way, yes, many of us can get to the point of not feeling life is worth it. I was lucky I had some reliable and well-trained people to go to for help. They were able to assist me out of that dark dingy basement of emotional gunk and muck, into my own light by using their internal light, as I now try and do with others. I am grateful for them and the guiding light that they gave to me in my time of need, as I now use my own light to show others out of their negativity; how to glean their own life and shine brightly for others in their lives. The trickle effect of positivity is a very powerful tool to have, helping yourself and another, directly or indirectly, out of the negative into the positive of one's life's journey.

That's where I believe Earth Angels come in; they pick us up as they move through their own basement of gunk and muck by the way in which they move through life's unchartered territories. I later realized my purpose was to be an earth angel going through the good and the bad of life helping who I can as I move through my own light. Shining, sweeping and lending a hand to help pick up others who are out there wanting to help themselves out of their dark well, or being stuck in their basement of gunk and muck; some just needing a beacon of light from someone to help them to keep going.

So, my hard work on myself in my younger years gleaning through all the negative parts of life, truly looking for what was good in each day, holding onto that and moving forward instead of being caught in my own basement of gunk and muck. Becoming resentful and feeling like I am slowly dying inside is not where I want my heart and soul to live. That doesn't mean I still don't have those moments. I don't allow those moments any more to be the focus of how I choose to portray my soul to others and myself. I would rather shine as best as I can and as often as I can, to be that ray of sunshine for myself and to be the beacon to others who need a guiding light.

With best regards, deepest feeling and many blessings,

DrG

Bibliography

Magee, Geri. "Woman to Woman." Success Breakthroughs. Jack Canfield, 2018.

Magee, Geri. "The Joys of Getting to Know Oneself." Warrior Women with Angel Wings: Illuminate your Joy. Dr. Sundi Sturgeon, 2018.

Magee, Geri. "Calling all Earth Angels, Healers and White Lighters: Awaken to Your Senses." Chapter title: "Sense-a-tional Readings." Reading Between the Signs. Jill Rhiannon, 2019.

Magee, Geri. "You are Your Own Sunshine." Warrior Women with Angel Wings: Gleaning the Positive from the Negative. Dr. Sundi Sturgeon, 2019.

Rose, Isabella. "Planting the Field of Dreams." Goodness Abounds: 365 True Stories of Loving Kindness. Ed. Jodi Chapman and Dan Teck. DandiLove Unlimited, 2017. 127.

Rose, Isabella. "Reconnecting to Oneness." 365 Life Shifts: Pivotal Moments That Changed Everything. Ed. Jodi Chapman and Dan Teck. DandiLove Unlimited, 2017, 94.

Rose, Isabella. "The Healing Power of Love." 365 Life Shifts: Pivotal Moments That Changed Everything. Ed. Jodi Chapman and Dan Teck. DandiLove Unlimited, 2017, 59.

Sturgeon, Sundi. Dr. Masaru Emoto, https://thewellnessenterprise.com/emoto/ 2017.

Sturgeon, Sundi. Quantum physics research material.
https://en.wikipedia.org/wiki/Quantum_mechanics

Tants, Karen. Mahayana Buddhism reference material:
https://www.patheos.com/library/mahayana-buddhism

Made in the USA
Lexington, KY
12 December 2019